THE FOUNDATION OF LITERACY

The Foundation
of Literacy
The Child's Acquisition of the
Alphabetic Principle

Brian Byrne
University of New England, Australia

Psychology Press
a member of the Taylor & Francis group

Copyright © 1998 by Psychology Press, Ltd.,
a member of the Taylor & Francis Group

Psychology Press Ltd., Publishers
27 Church Road
Hove
East Sussex, BN3 2FA
UK

British Library Cataloguing in Publication Data

A catalogue record for this book is available from the British Library

ISBN 0-86377-818-6
ISSN 0959-3977

Printed and bound in the UK by TJ International Ltd.

To the memory of my father, Cecil John Byrne, and to my mother, Barbara Byrne

Contents

Preface

I had several aims in mind in writing this book, and therefore several audiences in mind as well. First, I wanted to bring together in a single place the research that I and my colleagues at the University of New England have been conducting into the early stages of reading development. The record of that research is scattered across a variety of journal articles, book chapters and conference presentations. I believe that it tells a coherent enough story to warrant collecting between one set of covers. This monograph series in developmental psychology provided an opportunity to do just that. The research mostly uses the methods of experimental psychology, and therefore one intended audience is other experimental psychologists concerned with the reading process. Another is developmental psychologists interested in cognitive growth. A third is educational psychologists interested in the application of experimental methods to the classroom situation.

Second, I wanted to make a contribution to the debate about literacy education. To this end, I hope that the book is read by teacher educators and by teachers themselves. In writing with this audience in mind, I have had to make some decisions about the level of detail to include and the background knowledge that I could assume. Most educators have not been trained in experimental psychology, and as busy professionals they do not always have the time to wade through a mass of experimental results, statistical analyses, and the like. They may be more interested in a summary of the investigation and its implications than a full account of methods and data. However, I have decided not to spare the reader the research details, because I wanted to make as convincing a case as possible for conclusions presented in the final chapter. Above all, I wanted the case to be verifiable. This entailed laying out enough of the techniques and data for readers to be able to judge for themselves the merit of the conclusions. So, if I have erred as far as this audience is concerned, it is on the side of more rather than less detail. To help, however, each chapter ends with a summary, and a briefer summary begins the final chapter.

Readers *are* spared the level of detail required by journal and book editors. That is because, as mentioned, most of the research has already seen the light of day in those forums, and it can be checked in the original sources. For the most part, statistical analyses are presented only for data not previously published. I have repeated summary statistics where I thought they illuminated matters, and have tried to present enough of the procedural details to give a feel for what our subjects faced in the various studies.

I wanted to make this book as self-contained as possible, accessible to readers with only limited preparation in psycholinguistics, linguistics and writing systems, all of which enter the story somewhere. To this end, I have embedded short tutorials in relevant topics, in particular Learnability Theory (Chapter 1), levels of language structure (Chapter 2), and writing systems (Chapter 2). Readers familiar with these can, of course, skip them, and I apologise in advance for the oversimplifications and misrepresentations that inevitably occur when complex matters are treated in an abbreviated fashion. Readers who are not familiar with these topics may find some of the ideas elusive and some of the terminology opaque. I apologise, too, for this, though I do provide references to accessible accounts of all these matters, and interested readers can turn to them for help.

I have not, however, provided similar assistance with statistics, even though some readers will not be familiar with data analysis techniques. It is just too big a topic to include in a book like this, even briefly. I hope that the surrounding discussion will make clear what the analyses imply, and what their limitations are. Even so, complete statistical novices might be advised to read the kind of abbreviated introduction to statistical procedures that many introductory psychology texts supply. A useful one is to be found as Appendix 2 of Atkinson, Atkinson, Smith, Bem, and Nolen-Hoeksma (1996).

All of the above should alert the reader to the fact that this is a research monograph, focused on a particular research programme. It is not a full-scale literature survey. Naturally, other individuals' and groups' work is mentioned as it relates to the questions that our research addresses. But others with better filing systems than mine can do and have done a better job of reviewing current research in the area of early literacy development (I am thinking, for example, of Adams's [1990] masterful account of beginning to read, and of Share's [1995] comprehensive review of phonological processes in reading development).

No contribution to the psychological literature stems from just one person, and there are many people that I want to acknowledge. Knowing where to begin is easy; knowing where to end is harder. I start with Ruth Fielding-Barnsley, who has been part of this project almost from its inception. Her keen observations of learning and teaching processes, her skills in working with children, her sensitivity in dealing with educational professionals and parents, her excellent feel for the experimental process under challenging, real-life circumstances, and her first-rate conceptual input to the empirical work and its interpretation have contributed immeasurably to the project. Luise Ashley, too, has been very much part of the design and implementation of the programme, and has brought special skills with children, teaching, and language to our work. Others who have made important contributions to data collection include Ken Brookman, Barbara Hindson, Fiona King, Sarah Lawrence, Carol Mackay, Cara Newman, and Amanda White. Hilary Pollock's fine artwork formed the centrepiece of the intervention programme described in the book. One of my students, Deborah Loxton, took the trouble to point out terms and concepts which needed clearer definitions.

Many colleagues have discussed with me the ideas and methods behind the research. I am particularly grateful to Peter Bryant, Stephen Crain, Kerry Dunne, Linnea Ehri, Carol Fowler, Helen Fraser, the late Steve Johnson, Alvin Liberman, the late Isabelle Liberman, Richard Olson, Jeff Siegel, Donald Shankweiler, and Bruce Stevenson. Others have provided facilities either for research or for writing. They include Alvin Liberman, Michael Studdert-Kennedy and Carol Fowler, directors of Haskins Laboratories, Jerry Smith and Ron Growney, chairs at the Psychology Department of the University of Connecticut, and Peter Bryant and Susan Iverson of Oxford University's Psychology Department. Yet others have been more distant influences on the book as good teachers, and I mention in particular Lee Brooks of McMaster University, and much earlier, John Maze, Terry McMullen, and Phil Sutcliffe of Sydney University.

It was Peter Bryant who issued the initial invitation to contribute to this monograph series, and for that I am grateful. Professor Bryant also acted as a reviewer, as did Uta Frith, Alan Kennedy, and Rebecca Treiman. Each read the draft manuscript carefully and critically, and each made valuable suggestions for change. The final product is, I believe, better for the initial one having been subjected to their scrutiny.

The staff at Psychology Press have exhibited great patience in dealing with the typically tardy author. Michael Forster, Jane Charman, and Rachel Windwood were my earliest contacts there, while Paul Dukes and Rohays Perry have overseen the final stages of composition and production. For the courtesies and skills of all these folk I am also grateful.

Friends and relatives have provided support in various forms throughout the period of research and writing. Among them are Danièle Burckhardt, Sue and Brian Cunynghame, Gwen Johnson, and Sandra Miller.

The Australian Research Council has funded most of the research described in the book, and for its continued support I am most grateful. The University of Connecticut Foundation financially supported two periods of residency at that university, which furnished opportunities to deepen my understanding of linguistics and psycholinguistics. My own institution, the University of New England, has also provided funds through travel grants and research support, and, of course, the well-equipped base from which I work. Narell Godber and Chris Lisle, part of the staff of that base, have rendered expert service in the preparation of tables and figures. David Heap and Frank Niebling, also part of the staff, have made important contributions to data collection through their technical support.

To all of the people and organisations I have mentioned, and to others I have neglected to mention, many thanks.

Phonetic symbols from the International Phonetic Alphabet are used in the book. The ones that are not self-explanatory (that is, not ordinary English letters pronounced in the normal way) are: /æ/ as in cat; /ɒ/ as in dog; /ɛ/ as in den; /ɪ/ as in pin; /eɪ/ as in bait; /ʌ/ as in fun; /i/ as in need; /ʃ/ as in ship; /ʒ/ as in measure; /ʧ/ as in chase.

CHAPTER ONE

Definitions, phenomena, questions, and frameworks

DEFINING THE ALPHABETIC PRINCIPLE

The term *alphabetic principle* refers to the relatively straightforward idea that the letters that comprise our printed language stand for the individual sounds that comprise our spoken language. Consider two simple words of English, *dog* and *den*. Both of these have three letters. This is motivated by the fact that both have three sounds. Both start with the same letter. This is motivated by the fact that both start with the same sound. For the same reasons, *mad* ends with the letter these words start with, and shares its first and second letters with *man*. In general, whenever and wherever a particular sound occurs in a spoken word, it can be represented by a particular letter.

To readers of this book, literate adults all, the fact that *dog* and *den* each has three letters and the fact that each starts with the same letter are unremarkable ones—trivial even. Here, however, is what I want to demonstrate about the alphabetic principle in this book: *To apprentice readers, it is far from obvious why words like* dog *and* den *are written the way they are, and discovering why they are is not trivially easy. Children will not, for the most part, make the discovery unaided, and the consequences for literacy growth of not discovering the alphabetic principle are serious. It follows that instructional methods that assume that the alphabetic principle need not be a prime, early focus, that it is obvious or trivially easy to discover, are ill-founded.*

1

Readers familiar with phonology, phonetics, and speech science will note some oversimplifications in how I have defined the alphabetic principle. One is the use of the phrase *individual sounds*. It implies discrete packages of acoustic energy, but discreteness is not in fact a property of the elements of speech. Another oversimplification attends the adjective *same (sound)*. It implies invariance, such that, say, the vowels *a* in the words *mad* and *man* are acoustically identical. They are not. I recognise these and other shortcomings in my definition, and I will address the ways in which these are oversimplifications as we proceed. Indeed, the simplifications themselves may embody some of the reasons why some children find discovery of the alphabetic principle to be a difficult assignment, as we will see. But the definition will suffice for the moment; it successfully describes the core feature of an alphabetic writing system. This monograph is about how children come to understand that feature. It is also about the consequences of achieving, and not achieving, a grasp of the alphabetic principle.

Others will note that the definition also oversimplifies the nature of one version of an alphabetic writing system, English. It is true that in English *dog* has three sounds and three letters, but *ship* has three sounds and four letters and *ox* has three sounds and two letters. It is also true that the words *weather, whether,* and *wether* all sound the same but are spelled differently. Inconsistencies and irregularities in English spelling abound, and we consider some of these later in the book. Nevertheless, English is fundamentally an alphabetic language and thus furnishes proper material for a book about the child's discovery of the alphabetic principle.

DETECTING THE ALPHABETIC PRINCIPLE

For the most part, we will consider the alphabetic principle to be in place in children who can decode novel print sequences, exemplified by nonwords like *sut* and *yilt* that they could not have learned "by sight". Unless children know why writing has the form that it does, they are unlikely to be able to make sense of print sequences they have not seen before. But it needs to be said at the outset that children could in principle understand why *dog* and *den* are written the way they are and yet not be able to decode new words. Put the opposite way, a failure to decode does not necessarily mean that a child has failed to grasp the alphabetic principle. Indeed, we will see evidence that this dissociation may sometimes occur. Nevertheless, as I will argue, the ability to decode is a product of understanding the alphabetic principle, and it underpins literacy growth. Hence, decoding can be used as a touchstone for the presence of the alphabetic principle in children's minds.

Moreover, though this is rather obvious, children could know how to read *dog* and *den* but not understand why they are written the way they are. They could read them in roughly the same way as you and I read *$* and *&* and *%,* by rote, without relying on any links between the individual letters and individual sounds within the words. In the case of *&*, there *are* none of these "sublexical" links; for a given child reading *dog*, there may be none either. The word might have been learned as a whole pattern, for example.

WHY STUDY THE ACQUISITION OF THE ALPHABETIC PRINCIPLE?

The answer to the question of why we should study acquisition of the alphabetic principle may seem obvious: English is written alphabetically, and therefore the ability to decode it, an ability essential for reading English, is based on an appreciation of the alphabetic principle. Moreover, it follows from this that we should investigate the best way to teach the alphabetic principle. But it is important to note that the first claim, that people employ the alphabetic principle during reading, is an empirical rather than a logical one. It does not follow automatically from the fact that English itself employs an alphabet. We have already granted that it is possible in principle to read words and not know why they are written the way they are. A good test of this kind of "rote" reading would indeed be whether the person can decode nonwords. If they cannot, their success with real words is probably based on rote associations between printed and spoken words. Rote associations of this sort would seem to place high demands on visual memory, given that different words share many common letters and letter groups. But humans are pretty good at remembering, say, thousands of faces, which also share many overlapping features. We could also say that this kind of rote reading would place special demands on instruction, requiring a teacher to tell the child what each printed word says. But this observation does not amount to an argument that rote learning cannot occur. In fact, case reports document the existence of people who can read reasonably well but are simultaneously poor at decoding. There are not many of these reports, and reading performance may be seen to be compromised on close examination. Nevertheless, their existence indicates that decoding, the ability to pronounce unlearned letter strings, may not be necessary for reading real words and the texts made from them. For an example of this kind of case and a summary of others, see Stothard, Snowling, and Hulme (1996).

Assume for the moment, however, that understanding the alphabetic principle is basic to reading English. Then we can turn to the second part of my answer as to why we should study acquisition of the alphabetic principle, namely to discover the best way to teach it. But it is not a priori obvious that we need to teach it at all, at least if we mean by *teach* to provide children with direct instruction. Whether we need to do so for the alphabetic principle is also an empirical question. Alphabetic writing is simply a set of rules relating letters to sounds, and humans are rather good at learning rules without direct instruction. Spoken language is probably the best example of this: Speakers create sentences and discourses under the control of complex rules and principles that they have never been taught in any overt way. Similarly, readers may learn the rules for pronouncing novel strings of letters without being directly taught how to do so. Young children acquire the structures and rules of spoken language without conscious effort and without explicit instruction once they are in an environment where language is used in a meaningful way. So young readers might acquire the principles and rules underlying alphabetic script without conscious effort simply from learning to read meaningful words written alphabetically. It may be unnecessary, or even futile, to try to teach the alphabetic principle directly, as seems to be the case for the rules of spoken language.

Thus, reading real words does not logically require a grasp of the alphabetic principle, and even if it did, understanding the alphabetic principle does not logically depend on direct instruction. The existence and nature of any links among these processes is an empirical question. We began our work with the reasonable assumption that these links exist, supported of course by the available research evidence (for a recent and particularly comprehensive survey of this evidence, see Share, 1995). We believed, in other words, that reading in an alphabetic orthography and understanding its basic design principle go hand in hand, and that this understanding needs to be taught. The questions of how use, understanding, and acquisition are linked remains, however, fundamentally empirical.

AN EXERCISE

Let us now turn to an exercise that provides a phenomenological introduction to the topic of the book. Phenomenology might seem an odd way to start a monograph in the tradition of experimental psychology, but to us literate adults the alphabetic principle seems so patently obvious that we have difficulty appreciating that children might have any problem in discovering it. The exercise is designed to help us recreate why there may be a problem. Afterwards, we move onto more solid ground with a summary of experiments on adults, which, like the exercise, are meant as an analogue to acquisition of the alphabetic principle by children. Finally in this chapter, we firm up the issues raised to that point and the questions that will be addressed in the rest of the book. We do so by selecting a framework for questions about the acquisition of knowledge in general, namely a version of what has become known as *Learnability Theory*.

In the top panel of Fig. 1.1 there is a fragment of a new writing system. Each of the four symbols represents a consonant of English. Your task is to learn to read this new orthography by practising on the lower panel of Fig. 1.1. Simply say the phoneme corresponding to each symbol in turn. (You will have to pronounce /b/[1] and /p/ with a following vowel, as in "buh" and "puh".) At first, you will need to check back to the top part of the figure, but soon you should have the symbol-sound correspondences memorised. Keep practising until you are a fluent reader of this new orthography. Once you know the system, turn to Fig. 1.2 and try to answer the questions there.

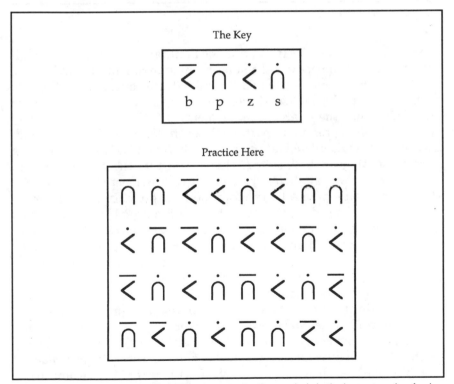

FIG. 1.1.   A new orthography. Practise pronouncing the symbols in the lower panel, referring to the key in the top panel. Continue practising until you are so fluent at saying the phoneme for each symbol that you can quickly read a whole line without referring to the key.

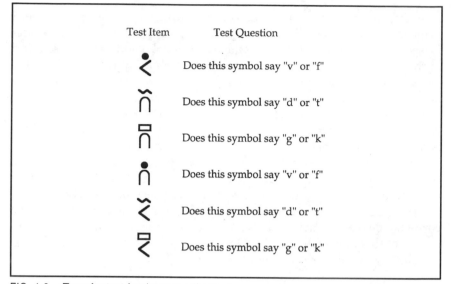

FIG. 1.2.   Transfer test for the new orthography.

Were you successful?[2] If you are not familiar with phonetics, and if you are like the majority of the subjects in experiments I will describe shortly, you probably were not successful with the questions in Fig. 1.2. In fact, you probably feel there are no sensible answers to those questions. But there are. The elements of the new orthography systematically represent properties of speech. Note that /b/ and /z/ share a symbol, <, as do /p/ and /s/, ⋂. In speech, /b/ and /z/ have something in common; they are both *voiced*. This means that the vocal chords are engaged when we say them. You can notice this most clearly with /z/. Hold your finger to your Adam's apple and say a prolonged /z/ (ZZZZZ...). Then say a prolonged /s/. Do you feel the difference? There is vibration in the larynx for /z/, but not for /s/; the sound /z/ is *voiced*, /s/ is *unvoiced*. Similarly, /b/ is voiced and /p/ is unvoiced. Put another way, /b/ and /z/ share the property of +*voice*, and /p/ and /s/ share the property of −*voice*.

Note, too, that except for voicing, /b/ and /p/ are made in identical ways, with the closed lips suddenly parting. They are created at the same *place* in the vocal cavity, they are *bilabials*. Similarly, /z/ and /s/ are made in identical ways (except for voicing), with a hissing sound from a groove made by the tongue at the alveolar ridge behind the top teeth. They are *alveolars*. The alveolar ridge is these sounds' *place of articulation*. The whole scheme (or the part of it that is relevant to our story) can be represented as in Fig. 1.3. The new writing system represents voicing and place: < for voiced sounds and ⋂ for unvoiced

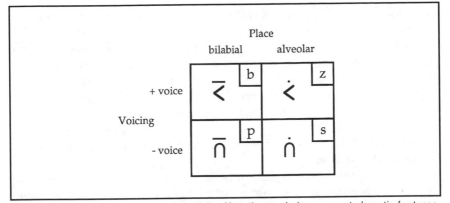

FIG. 1.3. Structure of the new orthography: How the symbols represent phonetic features. /b/ is a voiced bilabial /p/ is an unvoiced bilabial /z/ is a voiced alveolar /s/ is an unvoiced alveolar.

ones; – for bilabials and • for alveolars. Therefore, you could in principle successfully decide that the first symbol in Fig. 1.2 says /v/ rather than /f/ as long as (1) you had deduced that voicing was represented in the new orthography and (2) you realised that /v/ is the voiced member of the otherwise identical pair, /v/ and /f/. The fact that the upper part of the symbol was unfamiliar should not have proved an insurmountable difficulty because you could choose from the alternatives offered solely on the basis of voicing. Similarly, the second symbol in Fig. 1.2 must be /t/, the unvoiced member of the /d/ - /t/ pair, and so on.

I have challenged you with this exercise for several reasons. One is to help you appreciate the task facing the child learning to read. Three observations are pertinent as we try to put ourselves in the mental shoes of the apprentice reader. One is that writing is first and foremost about the sounds of language, not the meanings. It is mainly about the physical, not semantic, properties of speech. For literate adults, the meanings of written words are so immediately upon us that we tend to forget this fact. Words like *dog* and *cat* bring the creatures to mind straight away. With evocative words like *vomit* and *kiss*, the meaning response is even more obvious. If we can so readily bypass the fact that print records sounds, perhaps children might have problems realising this fact in the first place. In Chapter 2, I present evidence that this is precisely what happens.

A second observation is that writing systems represent speech at more than one level simultaneously. The symbols in Fig. 1.1 stand both for whole phonemes and for elements of phonemes. The very first symbol, for instance, represents /b/ when considered as an entire pattern, and the features of voicing and bilabiality when considered component by component. Duality of representation also holds for alphabetic writing. The visual pattern *dog,* for instance, represents both the entire word "dog" and the phonemes /d/, /ɒ/ and /g/. Formally, we can say that any writing system that is isomorphic with a particular level of speech is also isomorphic with all higher levels, where by "higher level" we mean the combination of elements from the initial level. So the writing in Fig. 1.1, whose elements represent phonetic features, also represents combinations of features, that is, phonemes. Alphabets, whose elements represent phonemes, also represent combinations of phonemes, that is, words.

The third observation that may help you to appreciate what the apprentice reader faces is that a learner can acquire the associations between a writing system and speech at a level other than the most fine-grained one available. This will be clear to you if you failed to make headway with the problems in Fig. 1.2. By the time you finished with the practice session in Fig. 1.1, you were a skilled reader of the orthography at the level of the phoneme. But, assuming you failed the transfer test of Fig. 1.2, you did not understand the writing system in all its detail, specifically the fact that it also represents phonetic features. Hence, you were unable to use the orthography productively in the structured transfer test I posed. Similarly, a child who knows what *dog* says solely at the word level would not be able to use the knowledge in a structured transfer test, for instance determining that *den* says "den" rather than "hen" if given the choice. Later, we will review evidence that learning of this restricted sort does occur in beginning readers. Children can learn to read words as wholes without grasping that parts of the print sequences stand for parts of the speech sequences. This, in turn, restricts their ability to decipher novel print sequences, even ones made up of the letters that are part of the words they have learned as wholes.

Another reason for the exercise is to introduce one of the experimental techniques I have used to explore the question of whether learners of writing systems automatically induce fine-grained levels of representation after being instructed in the system at a higher level. The technique, as will be obvious now, involves a *learning* stage followed by a *transfer* stage, with performance at transfer being used to explore what was learned in the first stage. In this chapter I report experiments with adults acquiring the orthography of Fig. 1.1, and in Chapters 2 and 3 I report analogous experiments with preliterate children learning to read word families. In the child's case, the one that is critical for this book, we ask the question foreshadowed earlier: Does knowledge of the principle that letters represent phonemes come "for free" from learning to read words written in an alphabetic script? We will see that in neither case, the adult's nor the child's, is there a guarantee that induction of the lowest level of representation will occur after fluency at a higher level is achieved.

The choice of learning-transfer paradigm and the decision to teach high-level correspondences were not simply made on the basis of experimental convenience. Rather, they are an attempt to reflect the learning environment and learning requirements that many children face in school. Certain approaches to reading instruction rely rather heavily on children's ability to induce enough about print-speech correspondences to be able, eventually, to read independently (Bloomfield & Barnhart, 1961). The children are taught to read whole words arranged in families, like *hand, band, sand*, with little in the way of specific instruction about individual letters and their corresponding sounds. The expectation is that regularities at the letter level will become clear with the creation of a "sight vocabulary" constructed in this systematic manner. In the "Whole Language" approach, similar assumptions appear to be made, in that direct instruction in letter-sound correspondences is mostly avoided as children learn to read words in meaningful contexts. The motivation for this aspect of Whole Language is provided by "the premise that there are strong parallels between reading acquisition and oral language acquisition. ... [Whole Language] stresses the ease and naturalness of oral language acquisition and suggests that learning to read would be equally natural and simple if meaning and purpose were emphasized. By extension, it is argued, if reading for meaning is the very purpose of the exercise, then isn't it misguided, even counterproductive, to focus the reader's attention on the individual letters and their sounds?" (Adams & Bruck, 1993, p.114).

Thus, my choice of high (word)-level correspondences as the target during the learning phase for the experiments with children mirrors the actual learning situation that some children face in school. And as reading *new* words is really a transfer task, the choice of transfer performance as the dependent variable is likewise justified by the school situation; children soon enough find themselves needing to figure out the pronunciation of words they have not previously seen in print.

Finally, the exercise affords the opportunity to introduce another concept that is important for our purposes, tacit knowledge. Let us assume that you readily learned to read the four symbols in Fig. 1.1 but failed to solve the puzzles in Fig. 1.2. You may object in your own defence that the properties of speech that the new orthography maps, voicing and place of articulation, are particularly obscure, so obscure that they do not enter into any mental computation we might engage in. But there is strong evidence that both of these properties are well known to you.

As voicing was the subject of the transfer test, we will focus on that. All phonemes of English are either voiced or unvoiced. When you speak, you betray tacit knowledge of voicing, for instance by changing how you say certain phonemes according to whether their neighbouring phonemes are voiced or not. To illustrate, the primary distinction between the words *nib* and *nip* is voicing (+ or –) of the final phoneme. But in addition the vowel [I] is held a little longer in *nib* than in *nip*. This is a general property of English pronunciation; vowels preceding voiced final segments are lengthened relative to ones preceding unvoiced final segments (compare *buzz* and *bus*, *dog* and *dock*, *mad* and *mat*, *save* and *safe*). Thus, when phonologists describe the rules of English pronunciation they cannot do so without acknowledging the voicing contrast. This is just another way of saying that you, the speaker, cannot pronounce English without acknowledging the voicing contrast; it is part of your tacit knowledge of the language.

Voicing is prominent in the perception of speech as well as in its production. One way to investigate what governs how people hear language is to make it hard for them to identify what they hear. The sounds that they can still distinguish are probably differentiated by properties that are prominent in normal speech perception. George Miller, who conducted pioneering studies of this sort, found that voicing is one of those prominent properties. Two sounds that are both either voiced or unvoiced are hard to tell apart (e.g., /b/ and /d/, or /p/ and /t/), but sounds on either side of the voicing divide (e.g., /b/ and /t/) are more easily distinguished. So the ear is acutely attuned to the presence or absence of voicing (Miller & Nicely, 1955).

The general point is that certain aspects of our knowledge are relatively inaccessible to consciousness, though, like the voicing contrast among phonemes, they influence how we act (speak and listen, in the present case). Most people could not describe the features that are the "atomic" elements of phonemes, like voicing. Even when confronted with a symbol system that honours them, as in our exercise, people apparently do not notice their existence. Therefore, one pertinent question for this monograph is whether preliterate children have anything other than tacit knowledge of the aspects of speech that alphabets honour, the phonemes. We will see that, for the most part, they do not.

THE EXERCISE REVISITED: EXPERIMENTAL DATA

I hope that the exercise convinced you that reaching a full understanding of how an orthographic system represents speech is not necessarily a straightforward matter. It is possible to learn to read in a writing system without fully grasping its fundamental structure. But the force of my arguments does not depend on your personal experience; there is a considerable amount of data to back them up. Here, then, is a summary of some experiments that will put my point on a firmer footing and that will introduce in more detail some of the experimental techniques we have used to explore analogous questions with children on the verge of discovering the alphabetic principle.

Learning without understanding.   The experiments are reported in Byrne (1984) and Byrne and Carroll (1989). In the basic experiment (Experiment 1, Byrne, 1984), university student subjects learned the orthography contained in Fig. 1.1 by methods similar to those used in our exercise and to a criterion of reasonable fluency. They were then presented with the transfer task represented in Fig. 1.2. The mean performance at transfer was exactly chance, 50%, showing that even though the subjects had learned to read the symbols they had not induced how the graphic elements represented the phonetic elements (voicing and place).

Interpreting failure.   At this point I want to introduce the problem of interpreting failure in psychological experiments, for failure is what we are faced with in the subjects' transfer performance in this basic experiment, and failure is often what we are faced with in experimental data from young children. The difficulty with using failure to explore psychological processes is that it is not always obvious why subjects in psychological experiments do fail. Most mental tasks involve many processes, and each one of these components could, in principle, be the culprit. To make this concrete, consider my interpretation of the basic experiment, that the subjects had not induced how orthography represents phonology. I drew this conclusion because of their failure at transfer. But it is plausible that the subjects had in fact worked out what the elements of the orthography stood for but that this knowledge did not show up at transfer. The transfer task may have been too hard in general (e.g., perhaps the subjects were confused by the new symbol). Maybe the subjects did not realise that the transfer pairs, such as /v/ and /f/, differed on the crucial voicing variable. Perhaps they simply were not trying very hard. From a methodological point of view, it is important to try to narrow down the reasons for failure by systematically eliminating possible but erroneous interpretations. The experiments now to be described were an attempt to home in on the correct interpretation of failure at transfer, and some of them provide a model for analogous control experiments that we later used in the research with children.

Control experiments.   In the first of these control experiments (Experiment 2, Byrne 1984), the subjects learned precisely the same symbols as in the previous experiment, but on this occasion their elements represented not phonetic features but the intrasyllabic components, onset and rime. The onset of a syllable is the initial consonant or consonant cluster, the *f* in *fit,* or *pl* in *plan.* The rime consists of the vowel and any succeeding consonants, *it* and *an* in *fit* and *plan,* respectively. As we will see in the next chapter, there is ample evidence that speakers of English are fully aware of this basic division of the syllable. The correspondences between the orthography and the phonology and an example of the transfer task for this experiment are shown in Fig. 1.4.

The adult subjects in this experiment were able to successfully transfer; mean score was 85%. So the failure shown by the subjects in the basic experiment could no longer be attributed to the transfer task being too difficult in a general sort of way. It is more plausible to blame it on inability to detect the fine-grained structure of the orthography in the first place.

In the report by Byrne and Carroll (1989) there are further control experiments, ones in which the dependent variable was changed from performance on the transfer task to performance during learning. Different performance measures do not always tell the same story about what is learned (Schacter, 1987). In particular, people can learn things

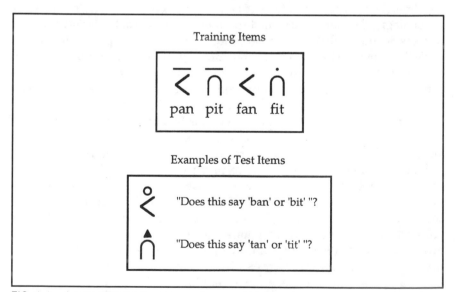

FIG. 1.4.   A new orthography representing onset and rime.

that do not show up in standard tests of learning like recall and recognition, or in transfer tests. The term "implicit learning" has been adopted for this phenomenon. So we reasoned that failure on the transfer task might exist alongside implicit learning of the orthography's structure.

The independent variable in these new experiments was consistency between the elements of the orthography and the phonology. How this was achieved is illustrated in Fig. 1.5. Subjects learned either the consistent or the inconsistent system. In the latter, voicing was inconsistently represented across the full set of orthographic symbols. In one experiment, all subjects initially learned the first four symbols in Fig. 1.5 until they could identify them flawlessly. Then the subjects were split into a Consistent and an Inconsistent group for acquisition of the final four symbols. If the subjects had implicitly learned how the writing system represented voicing while learning the first four symbols, the Inconsistent group should perform more poorly than the Consistent group, having been disrupted by the change in voicing representation. But in fact this did not happen. Both groups made similar numbers of errors in reaching criterion in the second stage of learning (as well as in the first). In other words, the reversal of how voicing was represented did not disrupt learning. This result strongly suggests that the subjects had not noticed the representation in the first place.

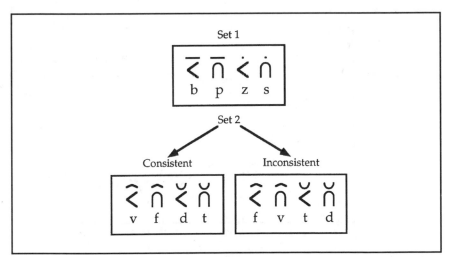

FIG. 1.5.   Schematic representation of consistent and inconsistent orthography/phonology correspondence. Subjects learned Set 1 followed by Set 2, which is either consistent or inconsistent with Set 1 in how voicing is represented. (Copyright © 1989 Psychonomic Society. Adapted with permission.)

The final control experiment is noteworthy not only because it confirms the conclusions we are able to draw from all of the data discussed so far—that subjects learn this orthography without fathoming its fine-grained structure—but also because it shows how persistent this "nonanalytic" learning can be. We trained two groups of subjects to use the orthography over several hours, with a total of 2400 exposures to symbol-phoneme pairs. One group had the consistent system, the other the inconsistent system (with voicing haphazardly represented). On this occasion we used as the dependent variable reaction time (RT) to produce the phoneme on the presentation of the symbol. If, during the relatively extensive exposure to this eight-symbol system that subjects faced, implicit learning of the basic structure was occurring, it should have become evident for the Consistent group as lower RTs. We knew from the work of Brooks (1977) that subjects can take advantage of regularity in a new writing system; RT becomes shorter after prolonged practice.

What actually happened can be seen in Fig. 1.6. There was no advantage for the Consistent group. Apparently they had not noticed the regular relationship between orthography and phonology. They certainly did not exploit it during learning. So all of the data I have presented point to the conclusion that it is quite possible to become a

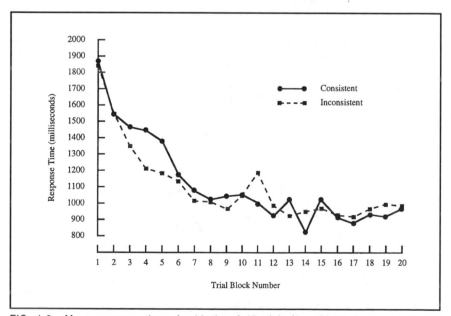

FIG. 1.6. Mean response times for blocks of 15 trials for subjects in consistent and inconsistent conditions. (Copyright © 1989 Psychonomic Society. Adapted with permission.)

reader in a writing system without registering its fine-grained structure, and that this state of affairs can hold despite quite considerable exposure to the system. We will see later that all of these things have been demonstrated to hold for children learning to read English.

Learning with understanding.   In the final three experiments of Byrne (1984), I attempted to discover what, if any, procedures might guarantee that my adult subjects could in fact learn the fundamental structure of the experimental writing system. The aim was to model, in the laboratory, instructional techniques that would help children discover the alphabetic principle during their early engagements with printed English. The experiments with the adults had demonstrated that mere confrontation with the orthography would not do the trick, so I tried the straightforward tactic of *telling* the subjects about the phonetic features of voicing and place and watching whether they then detected their representation in the writing system. The features were explained to the subjects in a short lecture delivered prior to presentation of the writing system, in much the same way as I explained them early in this chapter (recall the demonstration of voicing with the phonemes /z/ and /s/).

In the first of these direct-instruction experiments, the sounds used in the demonstration of voicing and place—/v/, /f/, /ʃ/ (the first sound in *ship*), /ʒ/ (the middle sound in *measure*)—were not the ones that subsequently appeared in the orthography (/b/, /p/, /z/, /s/). This turned out to be important. The salient finding of this experiment was that the minilecture did not help at all. Performance at transfer, 54 %, was no better than chance. It was as if our subjects' new-found knowledge about the structure of speech remained isolated from the very next activity in which they were engaged, learning a new writing system. We will have occasion to see that this phenomenon, isolated pockets of knowledge, crops up in children's performance as they learn about alphabetic writing.

In the next experiment, I made it easier to link insights into phonology and the acquisition of the orthography by using as examples in the minilecture the very phonemes that would soon turn up in the writing system, /b/, /p/, /z/, /s/. On this occasion, the transfer performance rose to 68%, significantly above the chance value of 50%. At last I had evidence of use and understanding being integrated. It appears that learners need not only to be told about the speech structures that the writing system portrays, but also to be told in a way that is as directly relevant as possible to the script they are learning. This conclusion was confirmed by the last experiment in this series, in which the subjects were told explicitly what the graphic symbols represented (voicing, place of articulation) after they had been given the minilecture on phonetic structure. They did not have to induce the relationship between graphs and features for themselves. On this occasion, transfer performance to the novel symbols was very high at 94%. Direct instruction works, at least in this laboratory analogue to reading acquisition.

Summary.   The results of this series of experiments tell us that people can learn high-level correspondences between graphic symbols and speech without simultaneously detecting basic-level correspondences, a state of affairs that can persist in the face of prolonged use of the orthography. They can, however, be rather readily taught these basic-level correspondences with well-targeted, direct instruction about the relevant elements of speech and how they are coded by the elements of print. We will see that these laboratory studies are a useful analogue to the acquisition of the alphabetic principle by children in classroom settings.

LEARNABILITY THEORY

To help us explore how the alphabetic principle is acquired, it will be useful to adopt a framework that provides a systematic way of probing the learning process. We would additionally like this framework to provide a way of capturing differences among children in how readily they discover the basic properties of alphabetic script. Differences do exist, and, importantly, they have implications for the overall development of literacy, as we will see. I suggest that a framework that meets these requirements is furnished by *Learnability Theory.*

Learnability Theory was developed as an approach to the study of language acquisition (Gold, 1967; see also Atkinson, 1992; Osherson, Stob, & Weinstein, 1985; Pinker, 1979). The full set of motivations for Learnability Theory is not important for our purposes, but one aspect of language acquisition that Learnability Theory addresses does have a counterpart in reading acquisition. It is the fact that the actual speech that children hear does not, of itself, unerringly lead them to the grammar of the language. The sentences they hear could be created by a number of underlying grammatical systems (see the sources cited for justification of this statement). Despite this, children soon settle on the correct, single grammar for their language. We will also see that the *printed* language that children encounter does not unerringly lead them to its fundamental nature. This is because a single writing system can reflect several levels of spoken language. Thus, in both speech and writing, children are faced with a discovery problem triggered by the existence of multiple possible bases for what they hear and see. These ideas will become clearer as we proceed; for the moment, they are meant to justify adopting Learnability Theory as a way of posing questions about reading development.

As well as the particular analogy between speech and writing just described, a more general justification for our use of Learnability Theory is the observation that it should be able to encompass all kinds of learning situations, not just spoken language (Pinker, 1990).

Learnability Theory partitions learning into subproblems, and I will adopt the following breakdown:

1. What is learned,
2. The nature of the learner,
3. A procedure for selecting the hypotheses that the learner adopts during learning,
4. A learning environment,
5. A criterion of success.

Under 1, we will consider the nature of writing systems in general, noting that different systems represent different levels of language; morpheme, syllable, or phoneme. We will focus on alphabetic systems in particular. We will assume that children do not know which of these orthographies they are facing, and that their task is to fathom which one it is.

Under 2, Learnability theorists consider the dispositions that the learners brings to the task. In spoken language acquisition, this might include a disposition to assume that the phrases and sentences they hear are not just one-off occurrences, but represent a sample from an infinite set generated by a finite rule system. Another disposition might be a mental set to try to fathom what the rule system is. With literacy acquisition, similar questions arise. We might wonder, for example, whether children who learn to recognise their first written word, their name perhaps, will automatically assume that all spoken words can be written down, or just names, or just *their* name. We might hypothesise a disposition to assume that writing systems are consistent; that, for example, a letter that represents the phoneme /s/ at the beginning of words also represents it at the end of words. Or that writing systems do not mix levels of representation, outlawing the possibility that some symbols stand for words and some stand for phonemes. These are empirical questions about which not much is known, but we will consider some of them in various parts of the book.

Under 3, the hypothesis selection procedure, specific hypotheses that the learner forms about Component 1, the nature of the system, are considered, as well as the way these hypotheses are chosen. The choice of hypotheses about the nature of a writing system is a real issue if for no other reason than, as we have seen, orthographies represent spoken language at more than one level. In other words, writing systems have more than one nature. So just as particular sentences of a spoken language are ambiguous with respect to the grammars that could generate them, so writing systems are ambiguous with respect to the levels of language they stand for. The child might hypothesise, for instance, that units of the writing system stand for the identifiably meaningful units of the spoken language, *morphemes*, and the child might do so because morphemes are somehow more prominent linguistic objects than the meaningless phonemes. I present some data on this in Chapter 2.

When language acquisitionists consider the learning environment (Component 4), they ask empirical questions such as whether children hear only well-formed sentences of the target language, and whether they receive useable feedback on the correctness of their own utterances. By and large, this quest is an attempt to characterise the learning environment, with the added assumption that it is effectively uniform for all children. In our case, we make no such assumption. In fact, we find different learning environments established by different educators, underpinned in part by different answers to other parts of the learnability puzzle. At various points throughout the book, we consider contrasting educational practices in light of the unfolding picture of how children acquire the alphabetic principle. Variation in the learning environment is one possible source of differences in how easily children acquire the alphabetic principle, and literacy in general. Other potential sites for individual differences include subproblems 2 (nature of the learner), and 3 (hypothesis selection procedure)—there is no a priori reason to assume that all children have the same dispositions or adopt the same hypotheses about the nature of written language.

The success criterion, Component 5 of Learnability Theory, is reached in spoken language acquisition when the learner no longer has to change any of the hypothesised rules in the face of incoming data (sentences). Our success criterion is of a different sort: It occurs when the apprentice reader can decipher any written word that turns up, whether encountered previously or not. This, for alphabetic writing systems, marks the discovery of the alphabetic principle.

LEARNABILITY THEORY AND
EDUCATIONAL RESEARCH

Any act of learning involves some contribution from the learner and some from the environment. The learner's contribution is what the learner brings to the task just by being the kind of creature it is with the kind of history it has. In Learnability Theory terms, this contribution is captured in Components 2 and 3, capacities and hypotheses. We can usefully think of it in the present context as children's untutored input to learning to read, what children can do all by themselves when faced with the world of print. Much of the research described in this book is an attempt to identify this input. The strategy we have generally adopted is to challenge children with a learning task and see what they make of it using their own resources.

Proceeding this way makes sense if one aim is to make recommendations about curriculum design, as is the case here. If we know what children bring to the task of learning to read (i.e., we understand Component 2, learning capacities, and Component 3, hypotheses about the system), and if we have a clear idea of what they *need* to know to be skilled readers (i.e., we understand Component 1, the nature of the system to be acquired, and Component 5, the criterion of success), we can work out by subtraction what the environment needs to supply. Put another way, spelling out what is in Components 2 and 3, the learner's contribution, will enable us to spell out what *ought* to be in Component 4, the learning environment, given Components 1 and 5. It is Component 4 that we, as teachers of literacy, have control over. It is important, therefore, to know how to construct it.

There are good, practical reasons for conducting educational research this way. It makes little sense to teach children things that they already know or that they can easily work out from other things we teach them. The school curriculum is already crowded enough. So, for example, if a child who learns to read just a few words written in an alphabetic script, *dog* and *den*, say, automatically comes to understand the fundamental principle of alphabetic writing, there is no point burdening the child with lengthy explanations about letter-sound correspondences. But it would be a more grievous error to overestimate the learner's own contribution. Then we risk omitting from the curriculum things that ought to be there. If we assume that a child who learns to read words in an alphabetic script will soon fathom the fundamental principles of that script, and in fact this does not occur, we leave the child stranded. All the child can do is to memorise the written forms of words, and, as we will see, this is a burdensome task that defeats apprentice readers.

It is easy to think of questions that could arise in a research programme with this orientation. For instance (and trivially), is it in the nature of children to assume that what they learn in the morning continues to hold in the afternoon? If not, we should be careful to explain that it does, or to teach reading both a.m. and p.m. More realistically, is it in the nature of children to assume that if *b* represents the first sound in *boy* it also represents the first sound in *ball*, or the last sound in *rub*? If not, we should be careful to make this clear, and to explain why. A good reading curriculum will be forged after the answers to these kinds of questions are known. There are many more of them than can be addressed in a single book, but my aim is to examine a few that I consider to be important and that have been the subject of controversy and research.

CHAPTER SUMMARY

The alphabetic principle can be defined as the fact that graphic symbols, our letters, represent the phonemes that constitute spoken language. They do this in a systematic way such that the same phoneme can be represented by the same letter wherever it occurs in a word.

Experiments with adults were reported, which showed that adults could learn to pronounce symbols in a novel writing system that stands for subphonetic features without understanding that it does so; they were aware of only one level of representation—the level of the integrated phoneme. These experiments illustrate the following important points about orthography: Writing represents the sounds of language at multiple levels; learners can become proficient readers of a writing system without fathoming its most basic relationship with speech, and this failure restricts the learner's prospects for utilising the system in novel circumstances.

Experiments with adults also showed that prior instruction in the properties of speech that a novel writing system represents can help them acquire useable knowledge of that system at that level of representation. The more directly targeted the instruction, the more thorough the acquisition.

The concepts and experimental methods used in the adult experiments guide our investigations of children's acquisition of the alphabetic principle. Learnability Theory also helps guide these investigations. It partitions the learning problem into components: (1) the nature of the system to be learned; (2) the nature of the learning processes available to the learner; (3) hypotheses the learner may entertain about the system; (4) the information available to the learner;

(5) the criterion of success. The empirical work to be described in this monograph sets as its goal the identification of the second and third components of Learnability Theory, learning processes and hypotheses. Proceeding this way will guide the delivery of the fourth component, the information the environment needs to supply to the child.

NOTES

1. I will use the standard notation of slash brackets to specify phonemes. I will use the International Phonetic Alphabet. Many of its symbols are the same as standard English symbols, and are self-explanatory. A list of nonstandard IPA symbols used in the book appears in the Preface.
2. The answers are /v/, /t/, /k/, /f/, /d/, /g/.

CHAPTER TWO

Children's initial hypotheses about alphabetic script

In the first chapter we defined the acquisition of the alphabetic principle as the detection of the most basic level at which alphabets correspond to spoken language, the level of the phoneme. We established that a given writing system may represent spoken language at more than one level (phonetic features as well as entire phonemes in the new orthography presented in that chapter), and that learners may not discover all the levels of representation even as they learn to use the orthography. The goal of the exercise in Chapter 1 was to recreate in us adults something of the potential problem that faces the child learning to use an alphabetic orthography, namely correctly identifying the basic level of representation. We found, perhaps through personal experience with the exercise, but certainly through the experiments I reported, that adults learning the new orthography did not routinely find its basic level. The question that we now begin to address is whether children have similar difficulties finding alphabetic writing's basic level.

A good place to start this investigation is with the ideas that children have about printed language as they first encounter it. If they come prepared, as it were, to notice how the letters of written words correspond to the phonemes of speech, then discovery of the alphabetic principle will be automatic once they begin to learn some printed words. If their initial ideas, however, encompass a different view of how print represents speech, then the alphabetic principle may remain obscure. What we are talking about is, in fact, Component 3 of Learnability Theory, the hypothesis formation process. Studying this process is a good place to start because what we as teachers should put in Component 4, the information provided by the environment, will depend in part on what is in Component 3. If the children's own hypotheses ensure that the alphabetic principle is obvious once printed language is encountered, there will be no need to explicitly teach it. If children's own hypotheses do not ensure this, there will be a need to teach the alphabetic principle.

In this chapter, therefore, we investigate the hypotheses that apprentice readers adopt in their early confrontations with alphabetic writing. This investigation will necessitate a brief tutorial on writing systems and the principles on which they are based because, as I will argue, the systems that have been created can be regarded as the candidate hypotheses that children might consider. That tutorial, in turn, necessitates another on levels of spoken language, because writing systems select from a menu determined by these levels. However, before embarking on these tutorials I need to point out that we join the story a little way along rather than at its very beginning. That is, I assume that children recognise in some way that script represents language. The reason that this is not the beginning of the story is that, according to Ferreiro's (1985, 1986) analysis, children need first to distinguish two modes of graphic representation, iconic (drawing) and noniconic (writing). Making that distinction is no mean feat, for several reasons. One is that both drawing and writing select the same kinds of lines (curves, straight lines, dots), so some other property must be registered as the distinguishing feature. Second, most writing systems comprise an arbitrary set of forms (e.g., the letters of English), which encode what is already an arbitrary set of forms, spoken words. (Speech is arbitrary in the sense that, except for those relatively rare instances of sound symbolism such as *woof* and *cock-a-doodle-do*, the sounds of words do not directly signal meanings.) Second-order arbitrariness probably challenges the human mind in special ways, as witnessed by the fact that writing is a relatively recent human invention, younger by far than spoken language (with its first-order arbitrariness). The work of Ferreiro plugs the gap in my coverage of the child's discovery of the alphabetic principle in that it presents an insightful analysis of these very earliest stages of emergent literacy as children learn that writing exists separately from drawing. We will examine further aspects of Ferreiro's work in more detail later in the chapter.

LEVELS OF SPOKEN LANGUAGE:
A BRIEF TUTORIAL

Spoken language provides quite a few sites to which graphic forms could attach, and in this section I define the levels that furnish these potential sites. This can only be the briefest description, and readers unfamiliar with elementary linguistics are referred to chapters on phonetics, phonology, and morphology in a quality introductory text such as Crowley, Lynch, Siegel, and Piau (1995). A partial summary of the scheme I outline is in Table 2.1.

Consider this sentence:

The spotted pig chased the unhappy cats.

The primary elements of the sentence are words, seven of them in this case. Words themselves are comprised of *morphemes*, which can be defined as the minimal meaning-bearing units of language. Sometimes a word is a single morpheme, like *pig* (referred to as a *free morpheme*), and sometimes it may be two or more morphemes. *Unhappy* is such a word, with *un* and *happy* its components. *Un* is the kind of morpheme that only occurs in conjunction with other morphemes *(unhealthy, unending*, but not, of course, the *un* of *under or uncle)*, and hence is known as a *bound morpheme. Happy*, which can be part of a sentence in its own right, is free. Other examples of polymorphemic words in our sentence are *spot(t) + ed, chase + ed*, and *cat + s.*

The remaining terms all refer to the sound system itself, not to meaning. At the highest level is the *syllable*, defined as a vowel flanked (optionally) by one or more consonants. So in our sample sentence, we can see that *the* is a single syllable, as is *pig, cats* and *chased* (despite its spelling, with two vowels), whereas *spotted* has two syllables and *unhappy* has three. Syllables are in turn divided into *onsets* and *rimes*, the onset being any consonants before the vowel, and the rime the vowel plus any succeeding consonants. In *pig, p* is the onset and *ig* is the rime. In *spot, sp* is the onset and *ot* is the rime. Within the word *unhappy*, *hap(p)* is a syllable, with *h* and *ap* as the onset and rime, respectively. The rime itself is subdivided into *peak*, which is usually the vowel, and *coda*, any following consonants, so that in the syllable *ask, a* is the peak and *sk* the coda. The elements that comprise the onset, peak, and coda are termed *phonemes*, and for clarity and consistency these are usually written using an internationally agreed set of symbols known as the International Phonetic Alphabet (IPA). Thus, *pig* has three phonemes, /p/, /ɪ/ and /g/. *Cats* would be symbolised /k/ /æ/ /t/ /ʊ/, chased as /ʧ/ /eɪ/

/s/ /t/, and so on. (Introductory linguistics textbooks provide versions of the IPA; see also Note 1 in Chapter 1, and the Preface.)

Phonemes are not the bedrock of the speech system because the way in which any particular phoneme is actually articulated can vary according to the speech context in which it occurs. In our test sentence, for instance, the /p/ in *pig* is pronounced differently from the /p/ in *spotted*. In *pig* it is *aspirated*, which means that it is followed by a brief silence during which a puff of air is expelled (try holding your finger in front of your mouth when you say *pig*). In *spotted*, /p/ is *unaspirated* (no puff of air).

Because the distinction I am drawing here—between a phoneme and the ways it is actually said—is not an easy one to grasp, it is worth looking at another example. Consider the words *ban* and *bad*. If you say them while holding your nose, you will notice that one, *ban*, comes out distorted while the other, *bad*, is relatively unaffected. This is because the vowel in *ban* is said in a different way from the vowel in *bad*—it is *nasalised*. You configure your vocal tract to allow air to vibrate in your nasal passages as well as your mouth—with the vowel in *bad*, the nasal passages are not involved. So blocking your nose affects how *ban* is said but not how *bad* is said. Yet another vowel, the one in *bat*, is said differently again. It is shorter in duration than either of the other two *a*s. Normally, of course, we do not notice these distinctions, and it is not them that make the difference in meaning among the three words. The difference in meaning is signalled by the different final phonemes, /n/, /d/, and /t/. It is the different final phonemes that also govern how each vowel is actually pronounced, a point to which we will return.

How a phoneme is articulated is not a random thing. It is determined by rules. There is a rule in English that governs whether sounds like /p/ are aspirated or not; roughly, they are aspirated if they begin a syllable, not otherwise. So aspiration occurs with *pig*, where /p/ begins the syllable, and not with *spotted*, where /s/ begins the syllable. There is also a rule in English that governs when vowels are nasalised. It is, roughly, when they precede another phoneme that is nasalised. The /n/ of *ban* is one such phoneme. And vowels are lengthened if they precede voiced sounds, like the /n/ of *ban* and the /d/ of *bad*, but not the /t/ of *bat*.

To take one final example of variation and rules, compare the way the two *the*s of our sentence are pronounced, with a neutral *schwa* vowel before *spotted*, and with a distinct "ee" before *unhappy*. The rule here is that the vowel in *the* is neutralised if the next word begins with a consonant, not otherwise.

Variations like these are pervasive throughout speech. They motivate the more concrete level of *phonetics*, as against the more abstract level of phonemics. The elements at the phonetic level, which we can think of as the way we actually articulate the phonemes, are called *phones*, so any phoneme can have one or more *phonetic realisations*. For instance, /p/ comes in aspirated and unaspirated versions, [pʰ] and [p] (by convention phones are placed in square brackets). These two pronunciations are known as *allophones* of the phoneme /p/. The vowel /æ/ has three allophones, [æ̃], [æ:], and [æ], corresponding to the way it is pronounced in *ban*, *bad*, and *bat*, respectively.

Finally, any phone can be classified by the articulatory gestures employed in its pronunciation. We have already seen something of this level of analysis in our discussion of voicing and place of articulation. The phone [p] is an *unvoiced bilabial* (among other things). The phone [s] is *an alveolar fricative*, a phrase which describes its place of articulation, the alveolar ridge, and its manner of articulation, forcing air through a groove, thereby establishing friction in the airstream. A full account of articulatory phonetics is, of course, well beyond the scope of this book: All we need to note now is that this level exists, and is a potential locus for a writing system.

Therefore, writing systems might represent spoken language at one (or more) of the following levels: word, morpheme, syllable, onset, rime, peak, coda, phoneme, phone, and articulatory feature. We will see that some of these levels do in fact figure in actual writing systems that people have created.

WRITING SYSTEMS: A BRIEF TUTORIAL

To make a start on the quest for the hypotheses that children may entertain about how print represents speech, we need some idea of what the potential hypotheses might be. A good place to begin with is actual writing systems that have been invented. These are, after all, the creations of human minds, and therefore in principle conceivable by children. What follows is an overview of the world's writing systems, interleaved with speculation about children's likely hypotheses about writing as they first approach it. We will largely follow the analysis provided by Sampson (1985), although it should be noted that scholars are not in perfect agreement about the development and nature of writing systems; see, for example, DeFrancis (1989) for a critical discussion of certain aspects of Sampson's ideas. As we will also see, however, differences that are important for an accurate historical and conceptual analysis of writing systems are not necessarily critical for our purposes, which simply involve developing a catalogue of conceivable orthographies.

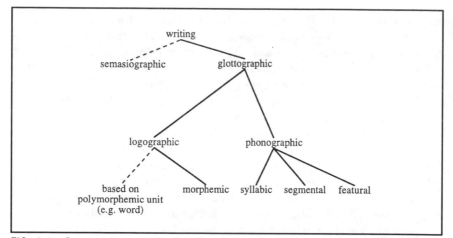

FIG. 2.1. Sampson's analysis of writing forms. Dashed lines represent forms whose inclusion as writing is open to doubt. (Adapted with permission.)

Sampson provides the classification of writing systems in Fig. 2.1. The major division, between *semasiographic* and *glottographic*, is akin to a distinction between the direct versus indirect (language-mediated) representation of ideas. Modern pictorial signs for international travellers, such as for male and female washrooms, passport checkpoints, and so on, which do not depend for their interpretation on knowing the language of the host country, are semasiographic. Sampson dismisses these systems as not being true writing, and we can follow him in that opinion and not further consider them. But it is worth noting that young children may well pass through a stage in which they hypothesise semiasography. Ferreiro (1986) documents children who believe, as they are read to from picture books, that when one reads, one reads the pictures.

Glottographic writing, which is a system that depends on the user knowing the language concerned because that is what it represents, subdivides into *logographic* and *phonographic*. In a pure logographic system, there are distinct graphic signs for each word, with no trace of the sounds of the language in its writing. Thus, two words that sound alike will not be written alike. If English were written entirely with symbols like &, $, £, =, and ©, it would be a logography. Sampson further suggests that a true logography, based on words rather than morphemes, probably does not exist. In such a system, there would be separate and physically unrelated pairs of signs for pairs of words like *dog* and *dogs*, *walk* and *walking*, *push* and *pushed*. In some languages, however, there are almost none of these inflectional processes to mark semantic notions like pluralisation, aspect, and tense (*s*, *ing*, *ed*). Each semantic element has its own, isolated morpheme. In these cases, a morphemic and a logographic system are indistinguishable. Sampson identifies Chinese as such a system, accounting for claims that it is a logography. But the broader picture of the world's writing systems suggests that Chinese should be classed morphemic. Inflectional languages that do not have phonographic scripts could in principle choose to be either logographic or morphemic, and it is in this context that Sampson claims logographies are not selected. Later in this chapter I provide evidence that children do not hypothesise a genuine logographic system even when one is compatible with the input they receive. They favour morphology over logography as the basis of written representation. Thus our data imply a cognitive basis for the absence of genuine logographies among the world's writing systems; the mind does not readily conceive of them.

It turns out that Chinese is not devoid of phonographic influences in its writing, as Sampson (1985) recognises and DeFrancis (1989) emphasises. Many words that are near homophones (sound alike) share a common graph (a *phonetic*), and are supplemented with a graph indicating the semantic category. To borrow one of Sampson's examples, the words for winnowing-basket and unicorn are almost homophonic, and the sign for unicorn is the sign for winnowing-basket plus the sign for deer (to be read as something like "the word for a four-legged animal that sounds like the word for winnowing-basket"). But this is not to say that pure morphemic systems could not exist, or, importantly for our purposes, that the human (and hence the child's) mind would not hypothesise morphology as the locus for written representation. For one thing, there are many Chinese words that show no detectable phonographic influence. For another, early writing systems, such as Sumerian, made extensive use of signs for morphemes (in fact, stylised descendants of pictorial signs), and only later did these signs themselves become the bases of phonographic writing. Third, even modern English has morphemic (nonphonographic) elements, such as the $, %, and & signs that we met in Chapter 1 and encountered earlier in this section. As Sampson (1985) points out, signs like these do not function to represent sequences of sounds—if they did, we should be able to write *land* as *l&* and *Andrew* as *&rew*. So, using as a criterion the principles that underlie orthographic systems created by humans, we can admit at least morphemic representation, and possibly logographic as well, as among the hypotheses that apprentice readers might consider as they endeavour to discover how writing encodes speech.

In Sampson's (1985) analysis, phonographic scripts, ones that record submorphemic elements, are realised at the levels of syllable, phoneme, and feature. The first two of these are quite uncontroversial. Japanese is the commonly quoted instance of a syllabic system (although more strictly it should be regarded as being based on the *mora*, a unit of timing; we will ignore this distinction). In fact, Japanese employs two sets of syllabic signs, derived from imported Chinese symbols, which supplied the earliest writing in Japan. (Japanese also continues to use logographic characters in what Sampson describes as a mixed system.) The essential property of a syllabary is illustrated in Fig. 2.2. The system does not acknowledge shared consonants or vowels in syllables, as can be seen from the absence of common graphic features representing a common vowel (the row) and a common consonant (the column). The syllable is bedrock (though see later comments on Japanese).

Before moving on to phonemic systems, it is appropriate to consider the subsyllabic but supraphonemic units of onset and rime as targets onto which orthography can map. In such a system, phonemes would only be given graphic representation when they occur as single-consonant onsets, and not otherwise. So the *s* in *sit* would have its own graph, and so would the *sp* in *spit,* but the two graphs would be unrelated. Similarly, the *it* of *sit* , as a rime, would also have a unique, single graph, unrelated to other rimes even if they shared a phoneme,

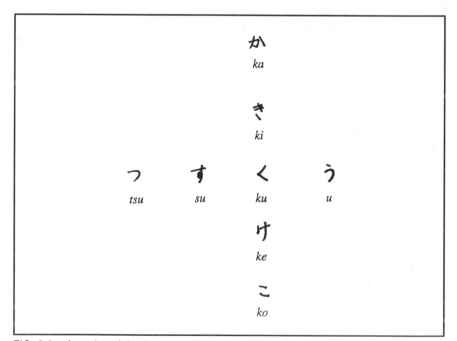

FIG. 2.2. A portion of the Japanese hiragana syllabary. (Prepared by Alice Kone.)

like *at* and *ip*. Obviously, languages with very large numbers of onsets and rimes, ones in which consonants were allowed to cluster freely, for instance, would require very large numbers of separate symbols, and hence be more cumbersome than purely phonemic systems. Languages where the number of onsets was not much greater than the number of consonants, or where the number of rimes was not much greater than the number of vowels, would be more likely candidates for writing based on onset and rime units.

As it turns out, instances of this kind of writing are not common. One exception to the general trend against onset/rime orthographies is the Hmong language. In a writing system invented by a local farmer during the 1950s, there are separate and apparently unrelated symbols for consonants and clusters created from these consonants; for /p/, /l/, and /pl/, for instance. One analysis of Hmong writing regarded sequences like /pl/ not as clusters but as complex consonants (Smalley, Vang, & Yang, 1990), in which case the writing is based on phonemes rather than onsets and rimes. However, others scholars prefer the onset/rime analysis (Poser, 1994; Ratliff, 1996), and Poser catalogues several other examples where symbols are determined by these larger subsyllabic units. Thus, though rare when considered against the opportunities that exist among the world's languages, writing based on onset and rimes does appear to exist. In the experiments that I describe later in this chapter, the possibility that children first entertain these units as the level at which print represents speech is not investigated, a decision that may be justified by the rarity of writing systems of this sort. However, future research should compare the prominence of onsets and rimes against other phonological levels in children's minds when investigating the order in which children consider how print does its work.

Alphabetic orthographies are basically phonemic. Stating things that way is both inclusive—the graphs record the phonemes of a language—and exclusive—the graphs do not record the phones of a language. Thus, in English, there is just one symbol for /p/, not separate symbols for [pʰ] and [p]. The phoneme /a/ in *ban*, *bad*, and *bat* is represented by a single letter, not one for each of its phonetic realisations. Nor are full vowels and their neutralised counterparts distinguished; there is just one spelling for *the*, however it is pronounced. In the context of our search for principles embodied in the world's writing systems, we are, of course, obliged to ask whether any language has a phonetic (as distinct from a phonemic) script. The answer appears to be no, almost. A few examples of subphonemic writing have been proposed. In Tamil, for example, the *velar nasal*, the sound we generally represent by *ng* as in *ring*, is allophonic with other nasals, yet in written Tamil it has its own letter, distinct from the one that represents the other nasals.

Some linguists have cast doubt on the genuineness of these instances, however, suggesting that factors like the desire to particularly mark the pronunciation for religious purposes may account for them. (I am grateful to Helen Fraser for information on this issue.) In any case, if phonetic writing exists at all, it is extremely rare, limited at most to isolated instances in a few languages. Thus, following our procedure of permitting the child to hypothesise principles of writing that are attested to in the world's orthographies, we would place phonetic representation low on, or perhaps absent from, the list. We will, however, allow the abstract unit of phoneme to be among the hypotheses.

Describing English as alphabetic, and hence phonemic, does not fully capture the systematic relationship between written and spoken language. There are also morphological influences on the spelling patterns of English words. For instance, even though the plural suffixes on *dogs* and *cats* are pronounced differently (/z/ and /s/, respectively), and even though we have two perfectly good letters for these different sounds, *z* and *s*, we elect to spell them both with the same letter. It is as if the spelling acknowledges the twin facts that there is just one morpheme (plural) and that how it is pronounced is predictable from the rest of the word (in particular, from the final sound of the stem, which, if voiced, requires the voiced form of the plural, /z/, and if unvoiced requires the unvoiced /s/). We can see the same process at work with the past tense inflection; a single spelling in the face of two (predictable) pronunciations. Thus, we have *pulled* (/d/) and *pushed* (/t/). The rule is very similar to the one governing how the plural is pronounced, namely the suffix is voiced following a voiced final segment in the stem, and unvoiced otherwise.

A *morphophonemic* system, as English can be called, ideally does not represent phonetic information that is predictable by rule. Note that English is not thoroughly morphophonemic. If it were, we would have plural spellings like *bushs* and *witchs*. Instead, we let the phonetic fact that a vowel is inserted prior to /s/ influence the orthographic form (*bushes* and *witches*), even though the phonetic form is predictable by rule (a vowel is inserted following a sibilant such as /ʃ/ or /tʃ/). If English were systematically morphophonemic, we would spell the prefixes of *improbable* and *intolerable* the same, as they are the same morpheme (meaning "not") and their pronunciations are predictable by rule (place of articulation of the prefix's nasal segment conforms to that of the following segment). Nevertheless, there are many places in English where the morphology does exert an influence. According to DeFrancis (1989), the majority of languages noted for their phonemic purity, such as German, Spanish, Finnish, Latin, and Greek, also show clear morphological influences. In High German, for instance, the singular and plural versions of the word for *dog*, *Hund* and *Hunde*, are both spelled with a *d* despite the fact that the final phone in *Hund* is the unvoiced /t/ whereas in the plural that segment is the voiced /d/. The same voicing alternation, ignored by the orthography, occurs in other words; for instance, *gelb* (the adjective *yellow* in constructions like *the rose is yellow*, pronounced /gɛlp/) and *gelbe* (the adjective *yellow* in constructions like *the yellow rose*, pronounced /gɛlbə/). (I am indebted to Kerry Dunne for these examples.) The persistent influence of morphology on orthography leads us to include it among the hypotheses that children consider when confronted with print. That is, we will let them entertain the possibility that writing maps onto morphological units of their spoken language.

If we leapfrog over the phonetic level (as genuine phonetic writing is virtually nonexistent), we come next to the level of phonetic features. We might immediately suspect that there have been no writing systems based on the feature, given the absence of ones based on the higher level of the phone. This appears to be the case, although traces of the feature matrix can be seen in some systems. For instance, Pitman shorthand represents phoneme pairs differing only in voicing, such as /b/ and /p/, and /g/ and /k/, by lines of the same orientation but different thickness (heavy for voiced, light for unvoiced). In addition, Korean script partly honours articulatory features, particularly place. So, for instance, the phones /t/, /tʰ/ and /n/ are based on the same form, out of respect for shared place of articulation at the alveolar ridge. This property of Korean came about because of a deliberate effort on the part of its creators to relate graph shapes to the position of the articulators during speech (DeFrancis, 1989). According to DeFrancis, however, the final result was not particularly systematic, and to describe the system as a whole as *featural*, as Sampson (1985) does, is not justified. Nor, according to these scholars, do literate Koreans generally appreciate the graphic relationships among letters, let alone the fact that resemblances are based on shared distinctive features.

There appear to be influences of the feature of voicing in the Japanese syllabary. The symbols for *ka* and *ga* are identical except for a *diacritic*, a small mark, placed next to the basic sign. The same diacritic distinguishes *sa* and *za*, *ta* and *da*, *ki* and *gi*, *si* and *zi*, and so on. According to DeFrancis (1989), the diacritic was created in the eleventh century as part of a move to reduce the number of signs in the syllabary (at the time, there were many more signs than there were syllables).

These isolated examples show two things: That phonetic features can influence orthographic form, and that their influence is sporadic. There are no writing systems built completely on a feature base, though such a system is logically possible (one would only have to elaborate the artificial orthography of Chapter 1 to represent all phonemes as collections of features, each with their own sign). Recall, too, the observation about Korean readers being unaware of the basis of their writing in shared features. If confirmed experimentally, this would accord with the finding, reported in Chapter 1, that English-speaking adults could not readily detect the mapping of symbols onto features, nor use features to speed acquisition of an orthography. Therefore, given the highly sporadic nature of featural influences on orthography, and given the experimental data of Chapter 1, I am inclined not to attribute to children the hypothesis that writing records the distinctive features of speech.

In summary, we have seen that the world's writing systems render up a series of contact points between graphic and linguistic elements. There is clear evidence that the morpheme, the syllable, and the phoneme provide anchor points for orthography, with weaker evidence

TABLE 2.1
Levels of spoken language providing potential sites of orthographic representation

Spoken language level	Example	Orthographc site?
	Units of meaning	
Word	pig chased cats	? (Ambiguous when words in a language are only single morphemes)
Morpheme	pig chase + ed cat + s un	Yes
	Units of sound	
Syllable	pig hap ed un	Yes
Onset, rime	sp + ot s + it b + e	Fragmentary
Phoneme	/p/ /s/ /i/	Yes
Phone	[p] p^h]	No ?
Feature	+ voice bilabial	Fragmentary

for a similar role for the word. The subsyllabic units of onset and rime form at least the partial basis for some scripts. Levels more detailed than the phoneme, namely the phone and the distinctive feature, either do not influence written form or have a marginal role at best. Based on the most widespread of the writing systems, we will attribute to the child the hypotheses that writing maps onto the levels of morpheme, syllable, and phoneme, and possibly word, and ask some further questions of detail about the hypothesis selection procedure. These questions, and some tentative answers to them, are addressed next.

THE HYPOTHESIS SELECTION PROCEDURE: A "RATIONAL" POSSIBILITY AND EMPIRICAL EVIDENCE

Recall that writing systems represent language simultaneously at several levels. We saw this in the experimental orthography used for the exercise in Chapter 1, and it is true for natural orthographies as well. Alphabets, for instance, systematically record syllables, morphemes, and words as well as phonemes. But note that this principle of multilevel representation is not symmetrical when considered in the context of representational grain. Fine-grain systems are also coarse-grain ones, but not vice versa. Japanese, a syllabary and therefore more coarse-grained than English, is not also an alphabet because it does not honour phonemes. English, however, as we have seen, does consistently represent syllables (and morphemes and words) as well as phonemes.

These observations suggest a systematic, rational procedure whereby children could, in principle, discover which level of writing system they are facing. The procedure is: *Assume that the system is the most fine-grained, and reset the assumption to the next most coarse level if in fact it is not fine-grained*. To put things more concretely: Children would do well to hypothesise that the writing system they face is an alphabet; if it is not, as will become evident when no systematic letter-phoneme relations are detected, they would move up a step to assume that it is a syllabary, then, if necessary, a morphography, etc. The reason that this is a rational way to proceed is that it guarantees finding the basic (= most fine-grained) level at which the system represents speech. If children learning to read Japanese hypothesise an alphabetic system, they will soon realise the mistake because words that share phonemes but not syllables will not look alike; that is, phonemes are not represented in the symbols. The children will then be motivated to reset the hypothesis and quickly settle on the correct level, a syllabary. In contrast, consider what happens when the initial assumption is that the system is coarse-grained. If children faced with an alphabetic system like English hypothesise that it is really a syllabary, they are not required to reset the hypothesis because English really *is* a syllabary (as well as an alphabet). So they may never discover the alphabetic nature of English. This will not mean that they will not be able to read the language. But it will mean that their memorisation task will be very great indeed because they will need to recognise the letter patterns corresponding to the syllables of English, numbering in the thousands. Similar logic applies if children believe that they are facing a word-based writing system, except that the predicament will be even worse. English, and all alphabetic systems, are also logographies, so nothing within the child will force the emergence of an alphabetic hypothesis. Now the number of separate letter groups to be memorised will be enormous, roughly identical to the number of words in the language (roughly, because there are homophones like *saw*, past tense of *see*, and *saw*, cutting implement).

In summary, Learnability dictates that it is better for children to think that the writing system they are asked to learn about is an alphabet rather than a higher-level scheme. Even if it is not, they will be motivated to shift to the correct level, a syllabary say, because there will be disconfirming evidence. If they initially think that they are learning a high-level system when they are learning one that is basically low-level, they will not have the same motivation to shift because low-level systems are in fact high-level ones as well. Disconfirming evidence will not be there.

It is important to stress that the procedure just described is presented as a *theoretical possibility*. It is how we might equip children's minds if we had control of them and wanted to ensure that they understood the nature of written language. It is not necessarily the procedure to which children actually adhere. Whether it is or not is an empirical question, one to which we now turn.

A good deal has already been learned about children's early ideas about written language by observing the children's attempts to make sense of print. Some of the most comprehensive work is by Ferreiro (1985, 1986). Her studies have not typically been experimental in nature, but, as we will see, they lead to similar conclusions to those from our experimental research.

Ferreiro suggests that children go through a series of stages in their early interactions with written language. First, they make sense of story reading by assuming "that when reading, one reads the pictures" (1986, p.17). Later, just a few months later in one case, Santiago, that Ferreiro (1986) describes in detail, they realise that reading derives from the print. But in trying to understand how writing and language relate, their first guesses are not about phonemes, or even about phonology at all. High-level units of language dominate. For instance, as children begin to identify individual letters as stable objects, they tend to think that each one represents an entire word. In the case of Santiago, each of his early collection of recognisable letters "belonged to" a familiar person—*S* for himself, *C* for Carmela, and so on. (There is no suggestion that he understood that S represented the initial sound in his own name.) Other evidence indicates that meaning is also an integral part of this early stage. For example, Ferreiro (1985) noticed that children represent quantity in quite direct ways. A child who uses a particular character to write "cat", a single letter or even a group of letters, may just repeat that character in order to represent several cats—three times for three cats, say. Other researchers, such as Landsmann and Levin (1987), have also reported that children think that quantity is marked by number of symbols. Levin and Korat (1993) found that young children learning Hebrew sought to represent semantic rather than phonological properties of words in spelling when the two conflicted. The children they studied tended, for example, to use more graphs to represent *coop*, a one-syllable word in Hebrew, than *chicken*, a four-syllable word. This tendency is also evident in reading-like tasks. Lundberg and Tornéus (1978) showed that Swedish four-year-olds favoured matching up the longer of two printed words with the name of the larger object—the short word for "arm", the longer word for "ambulance". Actual word length did not determine the children's choices.

According to Ferreiro (1985), children soon come to realise that equating each symbol with an entire word will not work—the total text, with its many letters, fails to coordinate with what is being said. In resolving their dilemma, the next point of contact that they acknowledge is at the level of the syllable. Children will use as many characters as there are syllables to write a word, because, Ferreiro claims, the first constituents of spoken words that are obvious to children are syllables. It is only later that they begin to coordinate their written productions and speech at the level of the individual segment, the phoneme. In Chapter 3 we will further consider the relative prominence of syllables and phonemes in speech. For the moment, the important point is that the progression that Ferreiro and others have observed—from high-level units of language to low-level ones—is in the opposite direction from the one that our "rational" child would pursue.

The experiments I shortly describe were designed to gather more evidence about children's early hypotheses about print. The question of whether children adopt the low-to-high progression that Learnability dictates takes on a particular importance in view of the fact that, according to some language acquisition researchers, this is precisely what happens as children learn their spoken language. In view of claims, to be presented in detail in Chapter 3, that learning to talk and learning to read follow much the same principles and paths, it is useful to examine places where the two aspects of acquisition can be directly compared. To do so first requires a brief explanation of how this principle is said to apply in spoken language.

The procedure to which our rational child might adhere in learning to read bears a resemblance to what is referred to as the *Subset Principle* in language acquisition. The Subset Principle is said to apply when the child is faced with figuring out the grammatical rule that underlies a particular sentence when there is more than one rule that could apply. If the rules are in a subset-superset relation (one is a more restrictive version of the other), then the child would select the "smallest" rule (the most restrictive one). If that decision is wrong, positive evidence in the form of new sentences of the language, which will conform to the "largest" rule as well as the smallest, will tell the child so. The grammar can then be adjusted. (See Pinker, 1990, for an accessible account of the Subset Principle in spoken language.) As implied earlier, in so far as these theorists are correct, the experiments to be described afford a test case for the claim that spoken and written language are governed by the same acquisition principles. Fine-grained writing systems as subsets of coarse-grained ones (an alphabet is also a syllabary, but not vice-versa). For a fuller discussion of these issues, see Byrne (1996).

One further digression before turning to the experiments: Is the idea of hypothesis formation a realistic way to pose questions about how children learn to read? After all, as a framework it runs counter to a long tradition in psychology whereby learning is seen as occurring unconsciously, as the result of the detection of correlations between stimuli and responses (print and speech, in this case). It runs counter, too, to modern embodiments of this tradition in the form of connectionist models of word identification, which have no obvious place for hypothesis formation (e.g., Seidenberg & McClelland, 1989). We will return to this question later with experimental evidence on whether induction of letter-phoneme relations inevitably occurs as children learn to pronounce words and word families written in an alphabetic orthography, and we will see that it does not. For the moment, however, consider this self-report from a disabled adult male reader who was asked to reflect back on his experiences in learning to read:

> I had learned symbols ... 1 and 2 and 3 ... so I wanted that
> for five-letter words ... I had this idea that ... I was going to

> know just by looking ... But there's no way you could possibly
> take all the words in the dictionary and just learn them by
> sight ... (Johnston, 1985, p.157).

This man's report already suggests to us that initial hypotheses are not unerringly fine-grained. He thought printed words represented speech in the same holistic way that numerals, 1, 2, and 3, represented number words, that is, logographically (cf. our earlier examples of $, %, and &, also read in this holistic way). But for present purposes the more important thing is that he did in fact make an assumption about how printed language worked; he did hypothesise about how print represents speech. It also appears that this hypothesis remained intact long enough for him to realise that it was a less than optimal way of learning to read. His history as a disabled reader also suggests that he did not find the key to pronouncing previously unseen words, further suggesting to us that induction is not a process automatically triggered by accumulating a sight vocabulary. So talk of hypothesis formation is not so unrealistic after all, and induction of the fine-grained structure of alphabetic writing does not always occur.

Anecdotal evidence of the kind just presented is useful, but not conclusive. Experimental examination of the processes involved in learning to read is needed to supplement personal experience. It is to evidence of this more rigorous kind that we now turn.

The experiments I summarise (see Byrne, 1996, for a full report) continued to use the transfer of training technique, this time with preschool children. Table 2.2 outlines the basic structure of the experiments, and a fuller description follows.

The strategy was to provide preliterate children with input that is compatible with more than one hypothesis about how alphabetic script represents speech and then to determine which hypothesis the children select. Specifically, preschoolers who knew no letters that were critical to the experiment were taught to read the pairs of words *hat* and *hats*, and *book* and *books*. In both cases, it is the letter *s* that discriminates the two words, and therefore we can be sure that a child who can reliably supply the correct pronunciation for the members of each pair has noticed something about that letter, as well as acquiring the basic associations. The question is, what has the child noticed about *s*? One possibility is that the letter "says" /s/. Another is that it adds a bound morpheme to the stem of the word. A third is that it represents a particular meaning change, to plurality, which is equivalent to noticing that *s* stands for the morpheme [plural]. Yet another is that it adds length to the word, which corresponds to the notion of plurality in an

TABLE 2.2
Schematic structure of experiments testing children's hypotheses about how print represents spoken language

Phase	Activity	Examples
Learning	Children learn to read pairs of words distinguished by print components that represent both a morpheme and a phoneme	1. hat, hats 2. small, smaller
Transfer I	Children are asked to distinguish new pairs of words distinguished by the print components where performance could be based on morphemic representation, phonological representation, ot both	1. cup, cups 2. mean, meaner
Transfer II	Children are asked to distinguish new pairs of words distinguished by the print components where performance could not be based on morphological representation	1. pur, purs ("purr") ("purse") 2. corn, corner

iconic way. The Learnability hypothesis selection procedure would predict the first of these possibilities, the phonemic value of s. This is because that association is the realisation of the alphabetic principle in this context, and Learnability dictates that children start with the assumption that they are faced with an alphabet.

Teaching each child to read each pair of words took about 10 minutes, around 20 minutes training in total. After the children had learned to pronounce the word pairs to a criterion of six errorless trials with each pair of words, they were challenged with a variety of transfer tests. The first was to decide which was which in other singular-plural pairs, like *cup* and *cups*, and *pot* and *pots*. For example, the pair *cup* and *cups* was placed in front of the child, he or she was told that one said "cup" and one said "cups", and was asked to point to the one that said "cup". This procedure was repeated with all the other singular-plural pairs, 12 of these test items in total. It turned out that the children could perform this task reliably. The mean score was 10.8 out of 12 (chance = 6). Of the 12 children in this experiment, 11 scored 9 or more out of 12, scores that indicate that the individual was not just guessing at the answer.[1] The point of this transfer was simply to check that children of this tender age, average 56 months, could in fact handle transfer tasks in this experimental setting.

The test does not disambiguate the candidate representative functions of the letter *s* because the transfer pairs are distinguished by an additional phoneme, an additional morpheme, and a change in meaning, just like the training pairs. But with a pair of words like *bug* and *bus*, or, in another experiment in the same series, *pur* ("purr") and *purs* ("purse"), the *s* plays only distinguishing phonological role. With this kind of transfer task, requiring sensitivity to the phonemic role of *s*, most of the children failed (in the *bug-bus* contrast, all 12 children scored less than 9, and the mean score was just 5.7; chance = 6). It appeared that the children had focused on the morphemic and/or semantic function of the letter to the exclusion of its phonemic role.

This conclusion was confirmed in another transfer test with the same children who had failed the *bug-bus* transfer, using pairs like *dog* and *dogs*, and *bed* and *beds*. Here the plural morpheme assumes the voiced value, /z/, different from the unvoiced /s/, which was how the plural was realised in the training items (*hats, books*). The children uniformly succeeded at transfer. They even performed above chance with items like *man* and *men*, *foot* and *feet*. Here, the plurals were written as *mans* and *foots*, but given the correct pronunciation by the experimenter.

In another experiment with a different group of preliterate preschoolers, training focused on the syllable *er* in the pairs of words *small* and *smaller* and *fat* and *fatter* (in the experiment, *fatter* was spelled *fater* to avoid confusions that might arise from the convention of doubling letters in adjectives with short vowels). Here, the *er* adds both a morpheme that adds meaning (referred to as the *comparative*) and a syllable. The first transfer test consisted of other pairs embodying the comparative contrast, like *mean* and *meaner*, and *cold* and *colder*. As with the plural transfers in the first experiment, the mean score on these items, at 9.1 out of 12, was significantly above the chance score of 6. But the children could not succeed with other pairs, distinguished by the syllable *er* but not by the comparative morpheme, like *corn* and *corner*, and *post* and *poster* (mean score 6.3). So once again we have evidence that children do not readily detect the phonological function of distinctive letter groups when they encounter systematic print-speech pairs, like *small* and *smaller*, or *hat* and *hats*. Instead, they seem to focus on aspects of meaning that present themselves.

In an experiment very similar to the previous one, we trained children to distinguish words on the basis of the superlative suffix *est*, as in *small/smallest* and *fat/fatest*. Children who did not know the pronunciation of the letter *s* were unable to use what they had learned in the training phase to help decode words where *est* played no morphological role, like *forest* and *harvest*. (The children who did know *s* did succeed with *forest*-type words, a finding that is consistent with data from Ehri and Wilce [1985] showing that apprentice readers can use partial letter information to decode words.) The result reinforces the conclusion that syllables do not present an easier target for graphemic representation than phonemes do.

In sum, the data show that preliterate children do not hypothesise that distinctive letters represent the sounds in words even when the fact that letters can do so is in plain view. It is not entirely clear from these data that children prefer to link the print to morphology; the semantic notions of plurality and intensity, or possibly word length corresponding iconically to these aspects of meaning, may be what children focus on. But the reluctance of children to create links with phonology does seem clear. Children do not seem to behave in accordance with the rational procedure of starting with the lowest level of representation as their hypothesis about print.

One caveat about this experimental series: In most of the experiments, a minority of children (up to two or three out of twelve) did succeed with the phonological transfer tasks even though they did not know the sounds of the critical letters prior to the experiment, as far as we could detect. We do not know what distinguishes these children, who appear to consider phonological elements as sites for graphic representation right from the start, from the majority. It is an important question, one which would remain ignored if we concentrated solely on average performances on children in experiments (see Note 1), and future research may provide the answer. We return to the issue of individual differences in Chapter 5.

Let us now place these results in the broader context of Learnability Theory, individual differences aside. Children who initially conceptualise English printed language as being based on a linguistic level higher than the phoneme, the morpheme say, are not in error. They just have not discovered the most basic level of representation. So there is no automatic self-correction mechanism built into their continued confrontations with writing, as there would be in the case of a Japanese child who thought that Japanese was alphabetic. It may even be difficult for a teacher to detect how the children have construed print if they have been able to memorise a suitably large number of morpheme-based print sequences. The situation will be exacerbated when the children can contrive to be told the pronunciation of printed words they have not previously encountered. Then, the pressure generated by having to work out these words' pronunciations, pressure that should force the children towards discovering the alphabetic principle that allows the decoding of novel words, will also be absent. In Learnability Theory terms, this particular combination of the children's hypotheses (print represents morphological units), the learning environment (a teacher who supplies new words' pronunciations), and the criterion of success (being able to read any word in a text) will conspire to keep the child ignorant of the basic nature of written English.

Is this a realistic scenario? Well, teachers sometimes comment on the apparent early progress of some children being followed by a decline beginning around Grade 2 or 3, generally associated with a substantial increase in the written vocabulary to which the children are now exposed. Up until then, the vocabulary is rather restricted, and teachers provide a lot of help for children as they seek to read new words. It is as if now memory capacity is beginning to fail, just what we would expect if the children were trying to remember how all of the morphemes of English look. More objectively, our research group has documented the reading progress of children who fail to develop strong decoding skills early in schooling (Byrne, Freebody, & Gates, 1992; Freebody & Byrne, 1988). The general picture is one in which some of these children perform at at least average levels up to the end of Grade 2 but show a decline starting in Grade 3. We will examine those data in more detail in Chapter 5. For the moment the point is that, on the assumption that decoding ability depends on discovery of the alphabetic principle, this picture of early success followed by later decline on the part of some children is consistent with what we expect from Learnability Theory considerations. Children whose initial hypotheses and instructional conditions hinder the discovery of the alphabetic principle and who are therefore forced to memorise morphemes are likely to begin faltering as memory demands for print sequences begin to increase substantially. This is despite the fact that they already memorised the pronunciations of many morphemes in their language. It just appears to be the case that learning to recognise an equally large number of printed words puts strains on the processes of learning and/or memorising that are different than the case for speech and that the task is too much for many children.

A final comment on these experiments on the hypotheses that children consider in their early encounters with print: It is sometimes claimed that young children are not analytic about printed words in their early encounters with them, that they simply learn words as wholes (see Byrne, 1992). This view has been criticised on empirical grounds (e.g., by Ehri, 1992). The experiments I have just described furnish another reason to be sceptical about such claims, and on this occasion with children as young as four years of age. Most children who participated displayed a keen analytic stance towards the words they were learning, parsing them into their morphemic constituents (stem +

plural, stem + comparative). To do this, they must have had the relevant morphological structures available as mental representations. It appears from our experiments that it is these meaning-based structures, or meaning in a more general way, that children recruit for making sense out of printed language.

The carriage of meaning is, of course, the stuff of printed language, just as it is of speech. But as we will see in later chapters, children need to discover that print does not represent meaning in a direct way, only by mediation through the structures of speech. Thus it would be inappropriate to use the evidence presented in this chapter, that children's analyses of print are oriented around meaning in the first instance, to support approaches to instruction that focus on meaning to the exclusion of phonological aspects of language. The debate about meaning's role in early instruction, already familiar to many readers, I am sure, will be subject to closer scrutiny in later chapters.

OTHER USES FOR LEARNABILITY THEORY

Finally, I want to suggest that we could exploit Learnability Theory to frame other questions about literacy development. Take the problem of consistency in English spelling, for instance. English is notorious for the number of exceptions to the rules, with words like *yacht*, *beautiful*, *island*, *aisle*, *once*, *have*, *of*, *was*, and so on. Many of these exception words are rather common, and occur inevitably in children's early texts (*Once upon a time, a beautiful yacht was sailing to a strange island ...*). Now imagine a child who has correctly detected the basic phonemic nature of English orthography and assumes that that is how writing works; it is alphabetic. The child is shown the word *was* (or *of*, or *yacht* ...) and the hypothesis suddenly is inadequate. Reverting to a morphological hypothesis might help, but no doubt by now that has been revealed as inadequate on other grounds (the fact that learning print patterns associated with morphemes does not enable the reader to figure out the pronunciation of new words, for example). We have little idea of how things might progress from there, but eventually the child does need to accept the confusing multiplicity of English orthography. On the way, a certain amount of cognitive confusion may occur, and in some children this may provoke a motivational decline that undermines further progress. That motivational problems that can attend reading development is understood: I am suggesting that some of them may have their origins in the hypotheses children form about the nature of print, and in the conceptual confusion that can emanate from the hypothesis-setting component of the learning process. We can presumably develop ways to help children through their confusions once we acknowledge their existence. Learnability Theory is a way of framing questions about the child's conceptions and therefore about the sources of the confusions.

As a second example of how Learnability Theory may be helpful, consider the possibility that once children accept that writing is about the sounds of language, they might expect it to honour the phonetic rather than the phonemic level. They might expect, for instance, that aspirated and unaspirated stops will have different letters. We have already dismissed this as a possibility in that the world's writing systems show little evidence of phonetic influence, but it is not entirely improbable that a child might consider it fleetingly, as early spelling attempts can reveal a high level of sensitivity to surface features of the sound system (Read, 1971). It should be possible to design experiments that detect a phonetic hypothesis. For example, if on first realising that writing represents sound children expect the *t* in *top* (aspirated) to require a different letter from the *t* in *stop* (unaspirated), they should be easier to train with different symbols in a spelling task than with the same symbol for both *t*s. But if using two symbols is a source of confusion, it would appear that they hypothesise phonemic representation right from the start. Work by Treiman (1993) does cast doubt on evidence that children try to represent phonetic detail—she considers it likely that the children analyse the underlying phonemes in a different way than adults do. Whatever the details, the point is that in researching reading acquisition from the point of view of Learnability Theory these questions arise quite naturally.

CHAPTER SUMMARY

Spoken language can be described in terms of levels, such as the word, morpheme, syllable, onset, rime, phoneme, phone, and distinctive feature. The world's written languages use some of these levels as sites for graphical representation, with the word, morpheme, syllable, and phoneme most widely represented. An important feature of writing systems is that fine-grained ones, such as the alphabet, also systematically represent speech levels of larger grain, such as the syllable and morpheme. Large-grained systems, however, do not systematically represent finer-grained phonological levels.

On Learnability grounds, it makes sense for children to first hypothesise the most fine-grained level of representation, namely the phoneme (and therefore the alphabet). That way, they can be guaranteed to settle on the correct level if their first assumption is incorrect just by resetting their hypothesis to the next level up. Starting with a coarse-grain hypothesis (e.g., that the writing system has morphemes as its basic level) may leave children stranded with that hypothesis; they will find evidence consistent with their hypothesis because fine-grained systems do also represent higher levels of language. Therefore, they will not be motivated to change their hypothesis.

Observations of children's early interactions with print and the experiments summarised in this chapter showed that most preliterate children do not first assume that English is an alphabet; they apparently hypothesise something higher, perhaps the morpheme, as the basic unit of representation. Preschoolers who learned to read a pair of written words distinguished by a letter representing both a morpheme and a phoneme, such as the *s* in the pair *hat/hats*, failed to notice the phonological role of the letter, focusing instead on its morphemic function. Thus, children do not follow the dictates of Learnability as they engage printed language.

Children who do not discover that alphabets have phonemes, and not morphemes, as the basic level are forced to memorise the pronunciation of large numbers of print sequences, a strategy that begins to take its toll as schooling progresses.

Learnability Theory may offer a way to frame other questions about literacy development, such as the effects of inconsistency in English spelling on children's progress in literacy and whether there is a stage in which children think that alphabets are responsive to phonetic variation.

NOTE

1. I mention both the average score and the number of children who could be considered to "pass" the transfer test because we need to be alert to the question of how representative effects are. Averages do not tell the whole story. Indeed, they can sometimes be quite misleading. We will see striking examples of that later. For example, in Chapter 3 we discover that young children are either quite good or quite poor at deciding whether two words begin with the same phoneme or not. If all we knew was the average score of our sample, we would conclude, erroneously, that children are more or less middling at this task. Throughout the book, I draw attention to both averages and numbers in pass and fail categories when this is appropriate.

    There is a second way in which the representativeness of effects is called into question. That is whether effects generalise over materials as well as people. There is some discussion about this in the present chapter for the experimental situation I am describing, but as yet we cannot be sure that the effects I report apply generally. In other cases, we need to be equally curious. For instance, children may be unable to say whether two words begin with the same phoneme when the phonemes in the test are, say, stop consonants, but perfectly able to do so when the phonemes are continuants. We need to keep these issues in mind when making claims about psychological processes.

CHAPTER THREE

Induction of the alphabetic principle?

In Chapter 2, we saw that young children do not unerringly detect that print represents phonological structures like phoneme and syllable even when the words the arc learning to read do mark those structures. Instead, the children seem tuned to detect systematic correspondences between print and meaning. The experiments I reported used rather special arrangements of words, but the results converged with more naturalistic observations of children, which also suggest a high sensitivity to meaning in early interactions with print. Nevertheless, those special arrangements are not usually replicated in real classrooms when children go to school; that is, children are not typically presented with stems and affixes as the reading material they are asked to work with. So even though I believe that the experiments in Chapter 2 (and Byrne, 1996) tell us something useful about how children approach printed language, their implications may be limited. In particular, the implication that children may not readily learn letter-phoneme correspondences as they accumulate a sight vocabulary might be limited to situations where components of printed words correspond to morphemic components as in *hat/s* and *small/er*. In a more natural reading vocabulary, where this condition does not hold, detection of letter-phoneme relations may be more straightforward.

In this chapter, therefore, we explore the powers of young children to induce the alphabetic principle as they acquire a reading vocabulary. We will in fact see that learning to read words written in an alphabetic script is no guarantee that the alphabetic basis of the writing becomes clear to the child. In the second part of the chapter we address the question of why the alphabetic principle may remain hidden to children as they acquire a reading vocabulary. Following the general research strategy identified in Chapter 1, we are interested in the resources that children themselves bring to achieving insights into how letters and letter groups represent phonemes. In Learnability Theory terms, we are focusing on Component 2, the nature of the learner, as we ask what capacities for induction and generalisation children can exercise once they have learned to read some words.

EXPECTATIONS ABOUT INDUCTION

What might we expect from children? For a start, we know that children can memorise the pronunciations of printed words at a young age, before school often enough. It is not uncommon for preschoolers to recognise signs in their environments, like *Stop, Exit,* or *McDonalds.* A sample of 126 preschool children, around four years of age, who were part of a study to be reviewed in the next chapter, could name an average of 2.7 out of 6 such signs (Byrne & Fielding-Barnsley, 1991). So we can ask whether children can exploit what they know about printed words to figure out the alphabetic principle, to come to realise, that is, that the individual letters stand for individual sounds. If they can do this, then there is little point in teaching the alphabetic principle; we might just as well teach words directly and let the child's inductive powers do the rest.

It is reasonable to expect that any inductive processes available to children would be most effective if the words they know form families, with some common phonemes and common letters, and other distinctive phonemes and distinctive letters. Learning to read a pair of contrasting words like *sat* and *mat* would provide a better basis for detecting the correspondence between symbols and sounds than a pair like *cat* and *dog.* Certainly, the information is there for the taking to a learner equipped with appropriately tuned inductive powers. The empirical question is whether children are so equipped.

Actually, psychology documents induction of this sort quite widely. There are many experiments showing that people, children included, can detect rule-governed relationships between stimuli and responses, often enough without being consciously aware of what those relationships are. Indeed, in the experiments I will describe shortly we will see evidence of successful induction on the part of children. In addition, with the emergence of connectionist models of learning, including models of learning to identify words (Seidenberg & McClelland, 1989), we now have formal ways of capturing this induction process, ones that do not rely for their operation on anything remotely resembling conscious awareness of the relationships between stimuli and responses. So there is reason to be optimistic that apprentice readers will make a good deal of progress in fathoming the alphabetic nature of English orthography by being taught to read, especially if they are taught groups of words thoughtfully arranged to expose letter-phoneme links.

"Whole Language": Expectations based on a theory of literacy learning. Our optimism about the induction process rests on another foundation, albeit less direct than the evidence just alluded to. A discussion of this other foundation provides the opportunity to introduce educational theory and practice into our investigation because it informs a currently influential viewpoint about how best to structure literacy teaching. This is the view that learning to read and learning to talk are governed by the same processes. In a nutshell, the reason that this aptly named "Whole Language" position gives credence to the idea of rapid induction of the principles of alphabetic orthography is that children make rapid progress in learning to talk on the basis of seemingly meagre information. Children quickly learn general rules and principles of grammar, word formation, and phonology after being exposed to a limited number of instances of these rules; that is, they readily induce the general from the particular. Spoken language acquisition must therefore rest on some powerful learning processes, and because, according to Whole Language theory, written language acquisition is governed by the same processes, we could expect similar, expeditious acquisition of fundamental features of writing.

Before I attempt to justify these assertions, let us hear from the major proponents of the Whole Language philosophy, Goodman and Goodman (1979):

> We believe that children learn to read and write *in the same way* and for the same reason that they learn to speak and listen. That way is to encounter language in use as a vehicle for communicating meaning. The reason is need. Language learning, whether oral or written, is motivated by the need to communicate, to understand and be understood (p.138, my italics).

Or consider this:

> Instruction does not teach children to read. Children are in no more need of being taught to read than they are of being taught to listen (p.140).

To these scholars, spoken and written language are all of a piece, except, presumably, for the input and output channels, ears and mouth for speech, eyes and hands for writing. This being the case, we should be able to take what we know about the timetable and processes for one type of language learning and apply it to the other.

We know that children learn to talk in a relatively short space of time, relative, that is, to the complexity of the learning task. Anyone who has tried to learn a new language as an adult will know how demanding it can be. Languages are full of subtle rules, many exceptions to these rules, and a very large stock of individual words. Yet young children appear to be untroubled in mastering all of this in a few short years. Consider vocabulary alone; Miller (1977) estimates that children have a vocabulary of around 13,000 words at age six, and of these nearly 8,000 are stems (recall that *walk* is a stem, *walking* is a derived word). Given that the first word appears at about age one, the simple arithmetic means that children learn, on average, seven new words every single day of their lives to age six, or over four new root words per day. The next year is even more of an achievement. By age seven, children know 12,400 roots, which translates to an acquisition rate of 12 per day. In the eighth year, the rate has moved up to over 14 per day. Given these speeds, it will come as no surprise that children are adept at learning an individual word on the basis of what seems to be a very scant encounter; hearing it just once in a situation where its meaning is clear from the context (Carey, 1982).

Documenting similar progress in learning the grammar of a language is not quite as easy in that it requires familiarity with modern syntactic theory. Briefly, however, a well-accepted view of how children learn the complexities of syntax in a few short years, at a time when they cannot tie their shoe-laces or do simple arithmetic, is that there is a series of "switches" that encode important features of the target language. These switches are waiting to be set by linguistic input that the child receives. When set, they determine a great deal about the grammar that the child is internalising. For example, languages vary in whether the word that gives a kind of phrase its special quality (the *head*) typically occurs first or last in the phrase. In prepositional phrases, like *under the bridge, on the boat*, the preposition (*under, on*) occurs first in English but last in Japanese (equivalent to *the bridge under, the boat on*). All that is needed is a few (maybe just one) phrases of this sort and not only does the child know that all prepositional phrases behave this way but also that other types of phrases in the language, like verb phases and adjectival phrases, are head first (or head last). So in Japanese verbs typically occur at the end of a verb phrase (equivalent, roughly, to saying *John Mary kissed*), something that children may not need to learn once they have learned about the setting for prepositional phrases. Perhaps something similar occurs as the child acquires the phonological system. For instance, recall that the voiceless stops, /p/, /t/, /k/, occur in aspirated and unaspirated versions in English. Rather than needing to learn these three alternations separately, the child might only need to notice the variation for one of the phonemes, say /p/, and then, aided by an innate idea of the "natural class", *voiceless stop*, automatically realise that the other two behave similarly.

Whether or not this "parameter setting" idea proves to be the correct way to characterise spoken language acquisition (see Atkinson, 1992, for a thorough if technical discussion), it does meet the requirement of explaining how children learn so much so quickly on the basis of incomplete information. Parameter setting is an attempt to flesh out the internal mechanisms that support rapid learning of language. The important point for present purposes is that there is a need for such a theory at all. The need springs from the facts of language acquisition, particularly its speed, so if this theory does not do the job, some other one will have to be found that does.

It is against this background that it is reasonable to expect rapid induction of important facts and principles of written language. The comparison with speech is not an overwhelming argument; it just provides a climate of expectation. Advocates of the Whole Language position should not be surprised to find that children can induce the alphabetic principle as they acquire a corpus of written words, given that these scholars ascribe to the acquisition of written language the powerful learning mechanisms that guide the acquisition of spoken language. Indeed, the Whole Language advocates would surely be surprised if matters turned out differently.

So we can turn to the experiments that we have run, which address the question of induction on the basis of printed word learning.

INDUCTION OF THE ALPHABETIC PRINCIPLE: EXPERIMENTAL DATA

The first experiment was conducted as part of the experimental series reported in the previous chapter (Byrne, 1996). Recall that those studies can be interpreted as showing that children focus on aspects of language other than phonology when they first meet systematic print-speech pairs. Recall also that in the experiments reported, the distinctive print elements and sequences, *s* and *er*, corresponded to separate morphemes, plural and comparative, respectively. Perhaps this feature of the design actually masked a potential focus on phonology; meaning-based elements of language such as morphemes might prove too strong attractors for the child to ignore. A more stringent test of the conclusion that children do not readily learn the phonological value of letters would be to strip the training phase of morphology and meaning as easily available sites for representation. Doing so would make the experiment more realistic because it is likely that children will confront word groups that share and contrast purely phonological elements rather than morphological ones, as in nursery rhymes, Dr Seuss stories, and the like. What we need to do, therefore, is to capture that kind of situation experimentally. If phonology still proved elusive, then it would not merely be a matter of competition from another source that is blocking phonological representation.

This first test (see Experiment 4, Byrne, 1996) was conducted by teaching the children a discrimination based on the letter *s* in which, in contrast to the *hat/hats* arrangement, there was no systematic morphological correlation. The 12 preschoolers, 5 males and 7 females, mean age 52 months, none of whom knew the letter *s*, learned to read *pur* ("purr")and *purs* ("purse") using a pair of pictures, a cat for *pur* and a purse for *purs*. The *s* was printed in red. The children were then taught the second pair, *dan* and *dans* ("Dan" and "dance") with the aid of drawings of a boy and a group of children dancing. They learned to discriminate and read these words to the criteria adopted for the earlier experiments, six errorless trials. In this learning phase there were relatively few errors, showing that a morphological contrast is not necessary for effective word learning.

The first set of transfer items consisted of *ey/eys* ("eye" "ice"), *ray/rays* ("ray" "race"), *play/plays* ("play" "place"), *die/dies* ("die" "dice"), *moo/moos* ("moo" "moose"), and *tray/trays* ("tray" "trace"). The *s* was also printed in red. Within each spoken word pair, one item is just the other one with a final /s/, as in the training pairs. (The distorted spelling is immaterial to preliterate four-year-olds.) The second transfer test consisted of the voiceless plurals used in the first two experiments (*bike/bikes, mat/mats, tap/taps, cup/cups, pot/pots*, and *lock/locks*).

The mean for the first generalisation (*ey/eys*, etc.) was 7.1, not significantly above the chance value of 6. The children did not seems to have induced that the distinctive *s* stood for /s/. They failed to hypothesise segmental representation even though it was available in the input and even though there was no competing morphological element corresponding to the discriminating print element.

Generalisation to plurals (*bike/bikes*, etc.) produced a mean score of 7.3, which was significantly above chance. However, only 3 of the 12 children had scores of 9 or more, the performance that can reasonably be regarded as being above chance at the level of the individual (the probability of scoring 9 or more out of 12 in a two-alternative choice by chance is about .07). Plausibly, these 3 children were exploiting an affinity between word length (or number of letters) and plurality, suggested as a possible mechanism earlier. But the majority of children performed at around chance level on plural generalisation as well as on the purely phonemic contrast. All in all, the data tell us that four-year-old preliterate children do not readily induce that print elements can represent phonemic elements even after learning a discrimination that depends on those very print and speech elements. They do not seem able to break words apart into their phonological constituents. Their failure to do so stands in marked contrast to case for morphological constituents, which young children do appear to notice and can link to print.

The distinctive letter in the experiment just reported was at the end of the word. We should try to give children every chance to show that they can induce phonological representation, and so placing the critical letter at the beginning of the words seems a sensible strategy. Initial sounds are likely to be more salient than final ones and hence more likely to provide a suitable environment for induction of the alphabetic principle. The next series of experiments all involved word-initial distinctive letters and segments.

In the first of these experiments (see Byrne, 1992, for full details), preschoolers learned to read the words *fat* and *bat*. The children were screened for knowledge of *f* and *b*, and the teaching schedule was the same as for previous experiments, namely a picture-matching stage and a reading stage. The children were then challenged with a forced-choice transfer test in which they were shown a word like *fun* and asked if it said "fun" or "bun". Other words in the transfer stage, besides *fun*'s companion, *bun*, were *fig, big, fell, bell, fin, bin*. Each was presented once in its appropriate forced-choice environment (e.g., does *bell* say "fell" or "bell"?), to a total of eight items. The transfer task differed from that used in the experiments described previously in that this time one written word was presented along with two spoken alternatives; in the other studies, two written words were shown to the child, who was asked to point to the one saying a single spoken word. This time, the transfer task was structured in the same way as in the experiments with adults learning the feature-based orthography described in Chapter 1.

Just like the subjects in the experiment testing whether adults could detect that the novel orthography recorded the voicing contrast, the children's performance, at 53%, was not significantly above chance. Just as in the adult experiments, it seems that the learners did not detect the fine-grained links between the graphic symbols and the phonological structures they represent. Had they done so, they would have had the resources to solve the transfer problems even though they could not read the test words themselves. We are again faced with a failure to induce the alphabetic principle.

Interpreting failure, again. We need to revisit the problems associated with interpreting failure in a psychology experiment, discussed in Chapter 1. In brief, they revolve around the fact that not being able to do something could be the product of the failure of any one (or two, or ...) of the processes involved in doing that thing. Common sense suggests that these problems might be magnified when children are the participants. So control experiments are needed to check on various alternative interpretations of the chance performance other than the one I favoured, that children will not readily induce letter-phoneme correspondences just by learning to read whole words.

In one of these control studies, slightly older children who already knew the sounds of the letters *f* and *b*, but who could not read the words from the transfer test (*fun, bun, fell*, etc.) were given the transfer test in the same format as the preschoolers without the prior acquisition stage of learning *fat* and *bat*. Although these children could not read the words "cold", they were uniformly successful in selecting the correct word when the decision space was constrained by the presentation of spoken alternatives, "fun", "bun", etc. Thus, we can be more confident that the children in the first study had not learned that *f* says /f/ and b says /b/; had they done so, they would have been in a similar position to the children in the control study and presumably similarly able to handle the transfer task.

Perhaps, in picking /f/ and /b/, we had accidentally selected phonemes that pose special problems for children. A survey of preschool children's knowledge of letter names and sounds, conducted in conjunction with this series of experiments, told us that the name of *f* was known to 23% of our sample (n = 77), and its sound to 7%. The analogous figures for *b* were 18% and 9%. In contrast, 49% and 33% of the children knew, respectively, the name and sound of *s*, and 37% and 19% of them knew the name and sound of *m*. These were the two best-known letters, and conceivably this was because the phonemes themselves are somehow more easily brought to the attention of children. Accordingly, a new experiment was run with these as the critical letters and phonemes, with care taken to ensure that only children who did not already know the letters participated. They were taught to read *sat* and *mat*, and tested for transfer to words like *sow* and *mow* ("does *mow* say 'sow' or 'mow'?"). But just as in the case of *fat* and *bat*, performance on transfer, 47% on this occasion, was not above chance. So the initial results cannot be attributed to the particular phonemes used.

Another way to check that the results of the first experiment in this series really mean that preschoolers do not readily learn letter-phoneme relations from systematic print-speech encounters with word pairs like *fat* and *bat* and *sat* and *mat* is to show that they *can* successfully transfer when units of language other than phonemes are involved. In one way, we have already seen that they do, in the experiments using morphological contrasts (Chapter 2). In another approach, using the same transfer of training methodology, preschoolers were taught to read pairs like *little boy* and *big boy*, and tested for transfer to pairs like *little cat, big cat, little fish* (also described in Byrne, 1992). Average transfer performance was reliably above chance, telling us that children as young as four can learn symbol-sound relations in an analytic fashion (that *little* says "little," *big* says "big") when the sounds are words. That is, the failures with *f* and *b* cannot be ascribed to a general inability to take stretches of language apart and to transfer new-found links between speech and print to partially new situations.

It would be even more convincing if the very same children who could successfully negotiate a word transfer task like the one just reported nevertheless had problems with the formally similar transfer with phonemes. To this end, a new group of children was taught the phrasal pairs *little boy / big boy*, this time using geometric symbols instead of actual printed words. The symbols, presented to the children as the writing of the Voltrons, a then-popular television alien civilisation, consisted of a red triangle (= *little*) plus a green square (= *boy*) for *little boy* and a blue circle (= *big*) plus the same green square for *big boy*. For the transfer test, a symbol pair like the red triangle (*little*) plus a yellow diamond would be shown, and the child asked if it said "little cat" or "big cat" (*little cat*). Particular interest centred on those children who performed confidently by reaching a preset pass criterion of 7/8 transfer items correct, 10 of the 13 children who began the experiment. These 10 were then taught the words *fat* and *bat*, using a new set of Voltron symbols (geometric forms were used so as not to confound the language-level difference, word and phoneme, with print distinctiveness, word pairs like *little boy / big boy*, versus single words, like *fat / bat*). The symbols had the same formal structure—a common final segment, this time representing the rime *at*, and distinctive initial segments, representing *f* and *b*. Transfer items included pairs like *fun* and *bun*, as before. None of the 10 children who had succeeded with transfer for the phrase pairs reached the pass criterion on transfer for *f* and *b*, and the average performance was only 45%. So the very same children who can induce how graphic symbols represent words in phrases cannot induce how graphic symbols represent phonemes in words. Children have inductive powers, but they do not appear to be able to exercise them over phonemic segments.

In the experiment just described, the move from words in phrases to phonemes in words involved three changes—words to phonemes, large to small units of language, and meaningful to meaningless units of language. Perhaps we could encourage children to detect how letters represent the small, meaningless unit of the phoneme if we introduced an intermediate learning stage using large, meaningless units. We did so by creating items from meaningless syllables. (I will describe evidence later in the chapter showing that children find it easier to notice syllables than individual phonemes.) The experiment is reported as Experiment 1 in Byrne and Fielding-Barnsley (1989). In the experiment, we began not with phrases like *little boy* but with compound nouns, *bus-stop* and *doorstop*. Pairs like *busman* and *doorman* were used for transfer. The second training set, the new stage, was the bisyllabic nonwords *bifsek* and *fotsek*, with pairs like *bifwub* and *fotwub* for transfer. (We continued to use geometric forms rather than printed words, and for this condition the children were told that Voltrons not only write funny, they talk funny as well.) Finally, the *fat/bat* condition was run; *fat* and *bat* as training items and pairs like *fun* and *bun* for transfer.

The experiment is outlined in Table 3.1. The central feature of the results is that children can learn symbols for components of compound nouns, bisyllabic words, and monosyllabic words, but can only transfer their knowledge of the symbols in the first two cases. In the third, where the critical symbols represent phonemes, they are unable to use their new-found knowledge in novel circumstances. The failure at the phoneme level cannot be due to a general difficulty with transfer in a symbol-learning context.

Together, these results make a strong case for attributing a special impenetrability to the phonemic level of language: As linguistic objects to map onto graphemic objects, phonemes lack the visibility of larger units such as words and even meaningless syllables. The experiments mirror the finding, reported in Chapter 1, that adults can readily enough learn to use a writing system that maps systematically onto a level of language, phonetic features in that case, but do not, at the same time, discover that basic level of isomorphism.

Let us consider the results in Learnability Theory terms. We know that children can induce the relationships between graphic symbols and linguistic objects because they can generalise to novel situations. So as we fill out the description of Component 2, the nature of the learner, we must include inductive powers. But these powers are limited; they do not operate over phonemes, at least as readily as they do over syllables, morphemes, parts of compound words, and words. We can attribute this limitation to Component 3, hypothesis-formation processes, saying that children will not hypothesise phonemes as targets for induction. This in itself does not explain why they will not, but at least it has given us a

TABLE 3.1
Structure of experiment testing preschoolers' transfer of training
with different language levels

	Stage		
	1: Compound nouns	*2: Syllables*	*3: Phonemes*
Subjects	17 preschool children	The 11 who passed transfer items in Stage 1	The 10 who passed transfer items in Stage 2
Learning set	Δ ⊗ bus-stop □ ⊗ doorstop	Δ ⊗ bifsek □ ⊗ fotsek	Δ ⊗ fat □ ⊗ bat
Examples of transfer items	Δ O busman or doorman? □ ★ busway or doorway?	Δ O bifwub or fotwub? □ ★ biflan or forlan	Δ O fun or bun? □ ★ fell or bell?
Result	11/17 children who reached criterion on learning set scored at least 7/8 on transfer items	10/11 children reached criterion on learning set, and all 10 scored at least 7/8 on transfer items	All 10 children reached criterion on learning set, but only 1 scored at least 7/8 on transfer items

Note: In the actual experiment, different symbols were used in each of the three stages.

framework for research. We know that we do not have to investigate the inductive process *per se*, just why it is not recruited when phonemes are part of the picture. Later in this chapter we will consider some reasons why these smallest of linguistic segments may be outside the scope of Component 3.

Ecological validity.   Do these experiments on induction tell us anything about what happens when children are exposed to a larger learning set? After all, in these studies the preschoolers only had to learn to read single pairs of items at a time, hardly a lot of grist for the learning mill. Admittedly, they could discover how print represents words and syllables with such scant exposure, and even a single sound when that sound coincided with a morphemic and/or semantic unit, the plural (Chapter 2). So the point that phonemes present special problems stands. But even phonemes might conceivably yield to the inductive process once larger numbers of words are learned.

One attempt to answer this question within the confines of the experimental techniques used in the other experiments involved increasing the learning set to four words, *fat bat fin bin* (Byrne, 1992,

Experiment 10). This may not seem to be a substantial increase in opportunities to acquire phoneme-letter links, but it certainly was a substantial increase in the task demands in terms of learning. Of the 14 preschoolers recruited for the experiment, 4 could not learn this set even after two days of training, and only 5 children learned the set without errors (this contrasts with the acquisition profile for 2-item sets like *fat* and *bat*, where errorless learning was commonplace). The error patterns showed that the items' confusability was the problem; 90% of the erroneous responses were words that shared either the initial consonant or the rime, "fat" for *fin*, or "bin" for *fin*, and only 10% were of the "bin" for *fat* type. If only chance factors were at work in determining error types, the respective figures would have been 67% and 33%. It is not clear whether the source of confusion was primarily visual or phonological, although the other evidence we have been considering, about children's insensitivity to phonemic structure, would suggest visual. In any case, under the pressure of confusion, it would surely benefit children to discover the fine-grained links between symbols and phonology.

Apparently the children were unable to do so, however, because the transfer performance to items like *fun* and *bun* was at chance level, just as when only two words were learned during the training phase. Moreover, the children failed in the other kind of transfer that is possible following acquisition of this set of four words, namely transfer based on the rime units. In this transfer, the children were presented with a word such as *pin*, and given the alternatives "pin" and "pat" as the responses. Had they learned the graphic representation for the rimes *in* and *at*, they could have solved the transfer problems. But again it seems they had not acquired the basic correspondences because transfer performance, at 55%, was not significantly above chance. So increasing the learning demands to the point where some children actually fail to acquire the set of words does not guarantee that the children who do successfully negotiate the training phase will discover how print corresponds to subsyllabic units of the speech stream.

The search for ecological validity beyond the confines of restricted experimental studies presents some problems. It would seem, in principle, a simple matter to extend the research upwards in age into real classrooms, locating some in which the alphabetic principle is directly taught and some in which it is deliberately avoided. Both instructional philosophies exist. There are those who maintain that the first steps in reading should be based on the component letters and sounds of words, and those who maintain that, from the beginning, meaning should be the focus of reading, with whole words rather than parts of them as the vehicle of instruction. This opposition of views has been referred to as the "Great Debate" (Adams, 1990; Chall, 1967). From the research standpoint, however, it is not a simple matter to adjudicate between the two positions in the classroom. Recall that we are interested in children's ability to induce grapheme-phoneme relations unaided when exposed to systematic print-speech pairings. Classrooms are not set up to meet the requirements of experimental psychologists (fortunately), so even ones that are committed to avoiding direct instruction in letter-sound relations may nevertheless furnish enough information in the form of alphabet charts and the like to disqualify themselves as testing grounds for unaided induction. It would take very careful scrutiny to ensure that they were really laboratories suitable for our purposes. Even then, we would lack control over, and in all likelihood much knowledge of, experiences outside the classroom that could inform the child about how the alphabet operates. Television programmes like *Sesame Street*, refrigerator letter magnets, lessons from older siblings, and a myriad of other experiences could reveal the workings of the alphabet to children. In brief, using classrooms as tests for the ecological validity of the conclusions we have drawn from the small-scale experiments is fraught with difficulties.

Therefore, it would be the more remarkable if evidence emerged that children in real classrooms did not appear to acquire the resources to read novel combinations of letters, which is what we have been treating as evidence for the alphabetic principle, despite likely exposure to aspects of written language at home and out in the community. As it turns out, such evidence does exist, in the form of a careful study by Seymour and Elder (1986). These authors followed the literacy progress of a whole class of Scottish kindergarten children who were being taught by a method that largely assumes that direct instruction in the alphabetic principle is not necessary (indeed, distracts from the true purpose of reading, which is to extract meaning from text). At the completion of the year's schooling, these children had respectable stocks of sight words (between 82 and 118 had been taught to various class subgroups by the end of the year). But the children lacked decoding abilities; they could not read words they had not been taught. The dominant response to unfamiliar words was to refuse to attempt them. Only 1 of the 24 children could read reasonable numbers of new words, and even he refused more words than he read. There were very few "neologisms", nonword responses that often occur when children are attempting to sound out words. There were very few regularisations (e.g., "off" for *of*), also a sign of a "sublexical translation procedure", as Seymour and Elder term decoding. Thus, the children appear not to have induced the relationships that hold between letters (and letter groups) and the sublexical components of words with sufficient clarity to generate pronunciations for novel letter sequences. So the phenomenon of learners acquiring a reading vocabulary but not grasping the fine-grained links between graphic and phonological elements is not limited to controlled laboratory demonstrations.

Individual case studies and group studies of children with reading disabilities supplement class-level research like Seymour and Elder's (1986). This research points to the existence of children who can learn written words by rote, sometimes with fair success, but who cannot read new words. Snowling (1987) reports on two children who could not read *any* novel words, despite having a repertoire of real words that they could identify. Snowling (1980) had earlier shown that, as a group, children characterised as dyslexic made some progress in reading as they got older by building up stocks of words that they knew by rote, but that this growth was not accompanied by corresponding growth in decoding skills, as evidenced by nonword reading. Larsen (1994; see Byrne, Fielding-Barnsley, Ashley, & Larsen, 1997) also found that third- and fourth-grade poor readers had word identification skills that were unrelated to the (low levels of) decoding skills that they had. For the children studied by Larsen, the growth in reading vocabulary that did occur was dependent on exposure to the words to a much greater extent that in competent readers from the same grades. The poor readers could not seem to use decoding skills to work out the pronunciation of new words and thereby add them to their reading stocks. Campbell and Butterworth (1985) describe a university-educated woman with high levels of word reading skill who performed very poorly when confronted with previously unseen print strings. The ones she could read may have been read by analogy to known words (e.g., *zolt* by analogy to *bolt*) rather than by analysis at the individual letter-sound level. Admittedly, cases like these may be marked by abnormal deficiencies in cognitive abilities, but their very existence tells us that acquiring a reading vocabulary is no guarantee that the alphabetic principle will be mastered. The totality of the evidence favours the view that an understanding of the basic organisation of alphabetic writing does not necessarily come for free as children learn to read words written using the alphabet.

A caveat.   The claim just made, that learning to read words does not automatically lead to insights into the alphabetic principle, is not the same as saying that children *cannot* acquire these insights just by learning to read words. It is entirely possible that this occurs, perhaps frequently. It is, of course, hard to know in any particular child's case whether unaided induction has occurred because of the difficulty of knowing how much information that child received from home, from school, and so on. Ethical considerations prevent us from conducting the experiment that would settle the matter, that is, isolating children from all sources of relevant knowledge other than the words they are learning and then testing for the presence of the alphabetic principle by asking the children to read novel words. We have come about as close to that as is reasonable in the experiments with four-year-olds who do not know the letters that are critical to the particular studies.

Language differences. Other languages may present better material for inducing letter-sound relations than English because they are more regular in spelling. German is one such language. "German orthography, in contrast to English orthography, shows a rather good fit between sound and graphemic representation. Specifically, there exists a rather straightforward mapping of the grapheme set onto the phoneme set" (Wimmer & Hummer, 1990, p.352). English, it will be recalled, presents the reader with numerous mismatches between grapheme and phoneme, as consideration of these short, common words demonstrates: *was, of, once, the, there, here, were, walk.* Research by Wimmer and Hummer indicates that right from the earliest stages children learning to read in German use a decoding strategy. First-grade children within six months of starting school generally have no difficulties in sounding out nonwords, and the correlation between word and nonword reading is very high. Although Seymour and Elder did not ask the children in their study to identify nonwords, it is a reasonable assumption that they would have performed very poorly; after all, they could not read real but unfamiliar words. Thus, the likely dissociation that the Scottish researchers found between word reading and a measure of decoding was not replicated in a sample of Austrian children. These latter children had mastered the alphabetic principle quickly.

Another set of observations by Wimmer's group (Wimmer, Landerl, Linortner, & Hummer, 1991) is also consistent with the idea that a transparent orthography can aid discovery of the alphabetic principle. That research showed that at the beginning of Grade 1 many children lacked significant levels of phonemic awareness but nevertheless had become successful readers and spellers of nonwords by the end of the grade.

However, the means whereby orthographic regularity influences literacy acquisition may not be direct but, rather, mediated by teaching strategy. Wimmer and Hummer (1990) point out that Austrian children receive systematic instruction in letter-sound relations, and "grapheme-phoneme correspondences are immediately used to identify words by sounding out the grapheme sequences. Due to the regularity of German orthography, such sound-out attempts quite generally result in successful word identification—at least when guided by teachers ...

[P]honemic transparency allows direct teaching of all relevant grapheme-phoneme correspondences and makes sounding out a successful word identification strategy" (p.367). Thus, these data from Austrian children do not constitute a test of the hypothesis that in a regularly written language children will induce the alphabetic principle unaided. The way the children are taught, conditioned by the regularity of the orthography and including direct instruction in letter-sound relations, may guarantee that children come to understand alphabetic coding and to use it in reading. As far as I am aware, the critical "experiment", in which children acquiring a regular writing system like German are taught with methods like those in the Seymour and Elder (1986) study, namely in ways that rely on the children discovering the alphabetic principle for themselves, has not been done. If it were, and if the children nevertheless quickly became competent readers of unfamiliar words, it would tell us that induction of the alphabetic principle can take place without direct instruction.

The written version of another language, Italian, is also more systematic in its grapheme-phoneme correspondences than English, and work by Cossu, Shankweiler, Liberman, and Gugliotta (1995) shows that Italian children also exhibit impressive decoding skills early in their school careers. Furthermore, a comparative analysis of American and Italian children's reading errors indicates that errors are determined in part by within-language aspects of orthographic regularity. American children make a high proportion of their mistakes on vowels; Italian children's vowel errors constitute a minority of their mistakes. In English, vowels are rather unsystematically spelled, mainly because the language has about a dozen vowel segments in speech to be represented by just five letters. Italian has only seven stressed vowels for five letters, and any given letter is only pronounced one way.

Cossu at al. (1995) indicate that reading instruction may be less geared to teaching grapheme correspondences than is the case in Austria. They tell us that "in the school selected for our study, reading is taught eclectically. None of the children experienced anything approximating a pure phonic or pure whole-word approach" (p.242). So these data may come closer to a test of the possibility that children can fathom alphabetic coding unaided. But without firm information on teaching practices, or without an experiment of the sort recommended earlier, we cannot be sure that this happens routinely in European school children learning regularly spelled languages. However, we need to remain alert to the possibility that the irregularity of English may be a source of confusion to children. A dawning grasp of the alphabetic principle, founded on induction over an accumulating stock of sight words, might be undermined by the failure of a phonemic hypothesis to fully fit the evidence, with frequently occurring words like of, was, once, and so on. That possibility has not received sufficient attention by researchers.

Despite all of this, it remains true that our experimental evidence clearly shows that induction over phonemic structures does not occur with anything approaching the ease of induction over other linguistic units—syllable, morpheme, and word. This initial hesitation may project into and be magnified by real educational settings, so that teaching schemes that assume inductive power on the part of children may leave them stranded, knowing by heart words they are frequently exposed to but unable to cope with anything new. The magnification of the faltering start may set in as a growing sense of inability leads to motivational decline, as seems to be the case with the adult nonreader from Johnston (1985), described earlier.

WHY DO PHONEMIC UNITS PRESENT PROBLEMS FOR THE INDUCTIVE PROCESS?

I suggest that there are two reasons why children do not automatically learn about phonemic representation when they learn to read alphabetically written words. One is that they do not hypothesise *any* level of phonological representation when they first confront print. That was the message of the experiments in Chapter 2, where the syllabic *er* proved no more tractable than the phonemic *s*. The second is that, even after children accept that writing is about phonology, phonemes present special problems not shared by syllables and other phonological units higher than the phoneme. So the basis of alphabet script is doubly difficult to fathom.

Form and meaning in language. The purpose of language is not to make noises but to express ideas, just as the purpose of walking is not to make rhythmic movements with the feet but to go places. Just as we walk without contemplating how we make the movements, so we talk without contemplating how we make the noises. Or at least that's true by the time we get to be good at these things, and by the time children begin to learn to read they are certainly good at talking. It may not only be that we do not concentrate on the structural properties of our activities, making noises and moving the feet, it may be that these things actually resist easy analysis. Try thinking about how you walk around a sharp corner. Do you turn the feet, swing one leg further than the other, engage in a controlled lurch? You probably cannot say, at least not without a lot of consideration. Rozin (1976) has in fact suggested that the very things that mark a species as special, and talking and walking upright must be numbered among the special characteristics of humans, are exactly the things that will be most inaccessible to conscious contemplation. This presumably is because they are so firmly grounded in the species' biology. So chess playing, a "complex" task but one that is not part of our inherent biology, is easier for us to analyse than walking, an "easy" task but species-identifying. Talking and listening are more like walking in this regard than playing chess.

Informally, we have seen dominance of meaning over form in studying children's judgements of phonological properties of words (more later). One child assured us that "tiger" and "clown" began with the same sound because they both could be found in the circus. The problem was not with the vocabulary of the inquiry because the same boy could make successful judgements based on syllables; that is, he could tell us that "pencil" and "penguin" started with the same sound (more on that later, also). Another boy, correctly this time, told us that "plane" and "train" rhymed because you could go places in both (this child could not tell us that other word pairs rhymed). Others have documented similar behaviour. For instance, during children's early apprenticeships as readers and writers, they expect a long thing, like *train*, to have a longer written word than a short thing, like *caterpillar*. They appear to be incapable of judging that a spoken word, like "mow", is shorter than a word that contains it, like "motorcycle", when there is no obvious semantic basis for the judgement (Landsmann & Levin, 1987; Levin & Korat, 1993; Lundberg & Tornéus, 1978; Rozin & Gleitman, 1977). It is precisely this orientation to language, with the focus on meaning, that is likely to block hypothesis formation centred on phonological properties of words, as documented in Chapter 2.

Some years ago, Peter Shea and I found that older children with reading problems showed an abnormal tendency to focus on words' meanings rather than forms (Byrne & Shea, 1979). We used an indirect method, capitalising on the fact that when people are asked to remember things, they get confused if the things are similar. In an experimental setting, remembering printed words that sound alike, such as *cap, map, cat, mat*, is more difficult that remembering words that are different, such as *cap, dog, fish, rug* (Conrad, 1964). Shankweiler, Liberman, Mark, Fowler, and Fischer (1979) had shown that this "acoustic confusability" effect actually applied less strongly to disabled readers, indicating that they relied less heavily on the sounds of the words in memory. In our study of memory processes, Shea and I adapted a method pioneered by Felzen and Anisfeld (1970), which used oral rather than written presentation of lists of words. The child listened to a continuous list that contained repeats and simply had to say whether each word had been presented earlier or not, an "old" versus "new" response. The list was structured so that some of the genuinely new words (not presented previously in the list) were similar to old ones in sound, such as *comb*, which rhymes with an earlier word *home*, and some were similar in meaning, such as *house*, which is semantically related to *home*. We found that second-graders who were reading at or above grade norms tended to respond "old" erroneously to both types of new items, rhyming (*comb*) and semantically related (*house*), following earlier presentation of *home*. In contrast, second-graders who were a year or more behind grade norms in reading made many semantic confusions (*house* for *home*), but no phonological confusions (*comb* for *home*). The poor readers appeared to emphasise meaning as the basis for memorising the words in the list, hence their tendency to confuse words that shared aspects of meaning. They appeared not to rely on sound as a memory code, at least not as strongly as good readers, hence their insensitivity to shared sounds.

One further aspect of this experiment deserves mention. It is that when we used nonwords like *jome*, *vome* (which rhymes with *jome*), and *fove* (which does not rhyme with *jome*) as the items, poor readers *did* show some acoustic confusions (saying yes to *vome* when it was presented for the first time following earlier presentations of *jome*). The poor readers did not make as many rhyming errors as the good readers did, but more than when real words were used. So children with reading difficulties are not incapable of directing their attention to the sounds of words, though their ability to do so may be impaired. But when meaning is available, that is where they orient. Perhaps, therefore, these particular children's difficulties can be traced back to a meaning focus in their early dealings with printed language, something that blocked their discovery of the fundamentally phonographic nature of writing.

Phonemes versus higher-level phonological units. The attraction of meaning cannot be the only reason why children have difficulty detecting that alphabetic script represents the phonemes of the language. Attentive readers will have noticed an apparent contradiction between the status of the syllable as portrayed in Chapter 2 and in Chapter 3. Recall from Chapter 2 that children were no more successful at discovering that the syllabic *er* and *est* stand for phonological units than the phonemic *s*. The children had learned to read pairs of words in which those letter patterns represented both morphemic and phonological units; *small/smaller, small/smallest, hat/hats*, for example. In none of the three cases did the children notice the phonological role of the letters. Apparently, therefore, the syllable was not a more prominent phonological target than the phoneme. Yet preschoolers *did* successfully learn symbols for the syllables *bif* and *fot* in the context of the meaningless words *bifsek* and *fotsek*, as documented in this chapter. The critical difference between these experiments may be the presence of a morphological attractor in the former and its absence in the latter. This could be seen as further testimony to the hold of meaning-based units of the language on children's early encounters with print. More importantly, recall that at the same time as the children were succeeding with the meaningless *bif* and *fot* they were failing with the equally meaningless *f* and *b* in the context of *fat* and *bat*. So phonemes are especially inaccessible as anchors for graphic symbols.

Our data line up nicely with observations about how easily children can make explicit judgements about the components of spoken words. The picture that emerges from the research is that the level of the linguistic unit is important, with syllables being easier than phonemes, and intrasyllabic units of onsets and rimes being intermediate between syllables and phonemes. One of the earliest reports came from Liberman, Shankweiler, Fischer, and Carter (1974), who showed that only 17% of kindergarteners could tap out the number of phonemes in a syllable whereas 48% could tap out the number of syllables in a word. Since then, other researchers have documented this disparity in accessibility between these two levels of phonology (e.g., Fox & Routh, 1975; Morais, Cluytens, & Alegria, 1984; Treiman & Zukowski, 1991). Treiman and Zukowski (1996) compared intrasyllabic units with syllables. They found that kindergarten and first-grade children were better at judging whether two spoken multisyllabic nonwords shared a sequence if the sequence was an entire syllable, such as "gan", than if the sequence was the rime part of a syllable, such as "arn" in "varn".

We compared rime-level units with phonemes. As part of a study to be described in the next chapter (Byrne & Fielding-Barnsley, 1991), we tested 128 preschoolers on their ability to judge that words contained the same sound. We did this with both rimes, in the form of rhyming words, and phonemes, in the form of initial and final consonants. In each case, we presented a target word and asked the children which of three other words either rhymed with it, or started (or ended) the same as it. An example of the rhyme test, which was modelled on procedures of Stanovich, Cunningham, and Cramer (1984), is *cat* (the target) and *hat, bed, clock* (the alternatives). An example of the initial phoneme test is *lamp* and *shoe, lock, heart,* and an example of the final phoneme test is *kite* and *sock, nose, boat.* In each type of test, instructions and practice made it clear to the children what was being asked of them, and in each case pictures of the targets and alternatives were provided to minimise memory load (see Fig. 3.1).

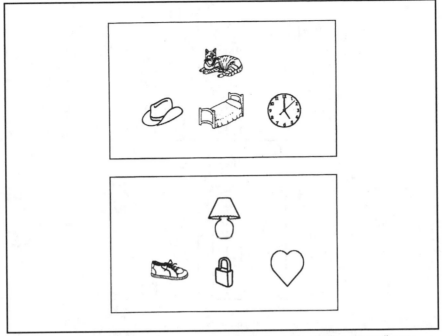

FIG. 3.1.   Examples of rhyme (upper panel) and phoneme identity (lower panel) tests.

We found that 60% of the children passed the rhyme test, with passing defined as a score of two-thirds or better (chance level is one in three correct responses). In contrast, just 29% passed phoneme identity. The absolute figure for phonemes is higher than the 17% obtained by Liberman et al. (1974), probably reflecting the different task demands and chance levels—it is not clear that there is any realistic chance level in a tapping task. Nevertheless, the results confirm that phonemes are less accessible components of the speech stream for children than higher-level units.

One additional feature of the results is noteworthy. In each case, rime and phoneme, there was a tendency for the children to fall into two categories, either at or close to maximum on the test or clustering around the chance value (see Fig. 3.2). In other words, preschool children seem either to be able to make identity judgements about phonological components of words or not. This tendency for children to fall into two clear ability groups persists into kindergarten, a year later, as shown in Fig. 3.3. This shows performance on a new test of phoneme identity, described in more detail in Chapter 5. For the moment, simply note that items in the test had a target item, like *pig*, and two alternatives, like *pool* and *beak*, from which the child had to choose the one starting the

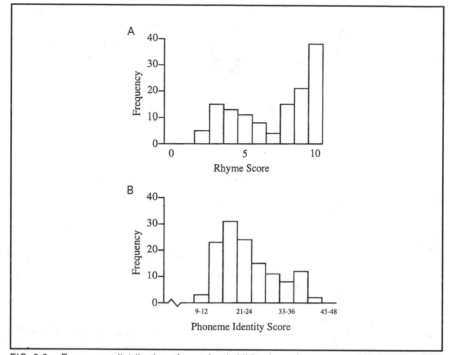

FIG. 3.2.   Frequency distribution of preschool children's performance on (A) rhyme and (B) phoneme identity tests. For the rhyme test, chance = 3.3; for the phoneme identity test, chance = 16.

same as the target. Chance therefore was at 50%, a score of 10 in this 20-item test. The bimodality of the distribution is clear; a minority of kindergarteners can do this test quite well, a majority not at all (i.e., at chance). Thus, judging from this sample of 220, most children begin their school careers not being able to reliably judge that two words begin with the same phoneme. It is precisely this level of linguistic structure that alphabets exploit.

To what can we attribute this special difficulty in making judgements about phonemes compared with higher-level phonological structures? Most of the available research has compared phonemes and syllables, and we will focus on that comparison. First, let us consider some important aspects of the machinery of speech, particularly properties that enable us to talk relatively quickly. The individual phonemes in a word are not pronounced as separate sounds, like beads on a string. In Fig. 3.4 you can see a spectrographic analysis of a speaker (me, actually) saying the word *man*. The signal is more or less continuous; there are no clear breaks between the "sounds".

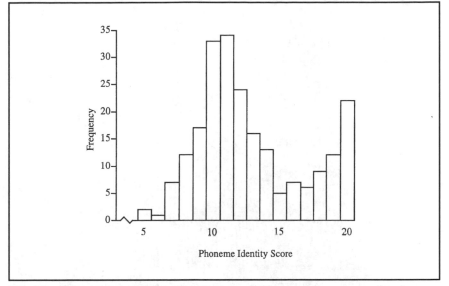

FIG. 3.3.   Frequency distribution of kindergarten children's performance on the phoneme identity test. Chance = 10. (Copyright © 1996 The Australian Psychological Society Ltd. Reprinted with permission.)

The individual phonemes are integrated into a single, seamless unit by a process known as *coarticulation*. This is the overlapping of the articulatory gestures involved in the different phonemes within a word. Thus when we say /s/ at the beginning of a word, we are already anticipating the shape of the following vowel. Consequently, how we say the /s/ will be different in "sat" than in "sit." This merging permits us to speak much faster than if we had to say each phoneme individually (as in overt spelling of a word, like "s...a...t"). Rapid but perfectly understandable speech may proceed at 20–25 phonemes per second, well beyond the rate at which we can recover the order and identity of nonspeech sounds. This ability is at the heart of our biological specialisation for language. In the words of Liberman and Liberman (1992, p. 351):

> Coarticulation has important consequences for speech perception ..., for it folds into a single segment of sound information about several successive phonemes, and so relaxes the constraint on the rate of perception imposed by the temporal resolving power of the ear. This produces a very complex relation between the sound and the phonological structure it conveys, but this considerable complication causes the listener no trouble; he or she has only to listen,

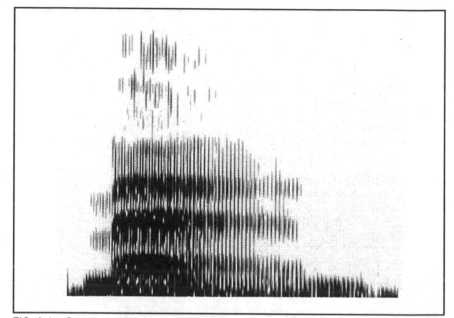

FIG. 3.4.   Spectogram of the word "man". Time is on the horizontal axis, frequency is on the vertical axis. The dark horizontal bands show concentrations of energy at particular frequencies.

> for the phonological specialisation parses the signal automatically, recovering the several coarticulated gestures that produced it ... Thus, the speech specialisation causes a word like *bag* to be coarticulated in a single, seamless piece of sound, even though it comprises three discrete phonemes. Given the automaticity of that specialisation, the constituent phonemes do not ordinarily rise to the level of awareness.

So the psychologically real unit, the phoneme, is part of an automatic and unconscious process, and furthermore is buried in the speech signal as a result of coarticulation. But syllables are more weighty units than individual phonemes. For one thing, vowels, the heart of syllables, are the most "sonorous" elements in speech. Sonority corresponds to the phonetic property of loudness, and in articulatory terms to the degree of vocal tract stricture (Carr, 1993; Selkirk, 1984). Syllables are frequently organised according to the "Sonority Sequencing Generalisation", which constrains segments closest to the vocalic peak to be more sonorous than ones further away (liquids and nasals, like /l/ and /n/, are more sonorous than obstruents, like /p/ and /t/, hence we have syllables like "plant", not "lpatn"). Thus, the vocalic nucleus of syllables is the most prominent component of the speech stream, and structural constraints imposed by the Sonority Sequencing Generalisation may give the syllable a regularity and therefore a stability not afforded individual phonemic segments, particularly consonants. Some speech scientists propose that listeners segment incoming speech into syllable-sized units (Massaro, 1974; Mehler, Dommergues, & Frauenfelder, 1981), although the preferred perceptual unit may be influenced by the speaker's language (Cutler, Mehler, Norris, & Segui, 1986). Overall, however, there is a case to be made for the prominence of the syllable in speech perception (Finney, Propopapas & Eimas, 1996).

Whatever the reason, it remains true that children are more aware of syllables than of phonemes, and can acquire syllable-symbol correspondences more readily than phoneme-symbol correspondences. Thus, the principle underlying alphabetic writing is obscured not only by being phonographic, but by being phonemic as well.

CHAPTER SUMMARY

Small-scale experiments with preschool children and larger-scale studies with kindergarten children tell us that learning to read words does not automatically generate an understanding of the alphabetic principle, evidence for which is the ability to decode novel print sequences. The failure of induction is not general; children can induce that graphic symbols represent parts of compound nouns, morphemes, and syllables, but at the same time they fail to detect phonemic representation. Thus, the inaccessibility of phonemes is partly due to the inaccessibility of *any* phonological structures as hypotheses for how print represents speech. But phonemes present special problems, possibly due to the way in which automatic and specialised processes govern speech production and perception, with coarticulation of phonemes a central feature of these processes.

The evidence presented does not accord with the idea that fundamental aspects of the reading process are mastered as quickly as fundamental aspects of spoken language. Children *can* rapidly learn to identify printed words, but understanding the alphabetic code used to write those words is far from an unerring consequence of reliable word identification.

In the terms of Learnability Theory, it is clear that Component 2, the characteristics of the learner, includes the ability to induce relationships between input, printed words, and output, their pronunciations. Children showed that kind of inductive power when they were able to decide that *bifwub* said "bifwub", having learned to read *bifsek* and *fotsek*. But induction seems to fail when the input-output relations map print onto phonemes, as the *fat/bat* example demonstrated. What are we to make of this apparent contradiction? Can we say that Component 2 both does and does not contain induction? Clearly, that is not an acceptable description of the learner. But I believe that we can resolve our dilemma by situating Component 3, the hypothesising process, before Component 2 as a kind of filter. The inductive powers that children demonstrably possess only operate over properties of the output that can be the subject of hypothesis. If, like the phoneme, they remain beyond the reach of hypothesis formation, they cannot be part of the induction process. I suggest that that is why children do not typically fathom the fundamental principle of alphabetic representation by themselves.

CHAPTER FOUR

Instruction in the alphabetic principle

So far we have established that it is possible for adults to learn a (novel) graphemic system without grasping the fine-grained level at which that system represents speech (Chapter 1). We have also established that children can be as prone to this kind of limited learning as adults (Chapter 3), and that one reason for children's susceptibility is their focus on meaning rather than sound in their early engagements with systematic print-speech pairings (Chapter 2). Another reason may be peculiar to alphabetic systems, namely the relative invisibility of phonemes in the speech stream. In Learnability Theory terms, some children fail to hypothesise that alphabets represent phonemes. That they can nevertheless read words is due to the fact that alphabets systematically represent language at coarse- as well as fine-grained levels.

We also established in Chapter 1 that adults' attention could be drawn to the phonological structures that the graphemic elements represent, and that this enabled them to grasp how the writing system works at its most basic level. The test for their understanding was the ability to make reliable judgements about partially novel graphemic structures. In this chapter, we will ask the same questions about children: Can their attention be directed to the phonological structures that alphabets represent, and does this enable them to grasp the alphabetic principle as evidenced by the ability to make sense of partially novel print sequences? The two questions are best separated because a positive answer to the first does not entail a positive answer to the second. The fact that we are asking the questions at all stems, of course, from the observation that children will not automatically discover the alphabetic principle by themselves. Under that circumstance, common sense tells us that they need to be taught about it. But how best to do so? In seeking an answer we are beginning to research Component 4 of Learnability Thoory, the information available to the learner.

ANALYSING SUCCESSFUL DECODING

To guide research into how to teach the alphabetic principle and how to decode novel words, we can start by analysing what a successful act of decoding requires. To keep matters simple, we will consider the restricted kind of decoding used in most of the experiments so far reported, namely deciding between two alternatives for the pronunciation of a printed word not previously encountered. Recall that the child was challenged with this task after learning to read pairs of words that differed by just one letter.

Thus, children are asked whether *fun* says "fun" or "bun" after learning to reliably distinguish *fat* and *bat*. To do so, they need first to have established a link between *f* and /f/ in the context of *fat* during the acquisition phase of the experiment. This, in turn, requires recognition of the separate status of /f/ in /fæt/. (I assume that children have no difficulty in noticing the separate status of the printed *f* in *fat*. Because the only visual property that distinguishes *fat* and *bat* is *f* versus *b* and the children in our experiments learned to discriminate *fat* and *bat* quite readily, this seems a safe assumption. The reason why successful acquisition of the word pair does not also necessarily mean that the independent status of /f/ has been noticed is that the distinctive letter may have been linked to the word as a whole, e.g., to its pronunciation as an integrated articulatory sequence or to its meaning entry in the mental lexicon.) Finally, children need to recognise the identity of the /f/ in /fæt/ and the /f/ in /fʌn/. If all that they know is that *f* says /f/ in /fæt/, they will not be able to select /fʌn/ in the transfer task.

The first of the requirements just catalogued is letter-phoneme knowledge, knowing that *f* "says" /f/. The second two requirements are aspects of what has become known as *phonemic awareness*. Understanding that /f/ is a psychologically discrete component of a word is the problem of *phoneme segmentation*. We saw in the previous chapter why segmentation is a problem; it is because words are articulated in an integrated way, with the overlapping and merging of gestures. Understanding that two words begin with the same phoneme, /f/ in this example, is the problem of *phoneme invariance*. Understanding that the /f/ in /fæt/ and the /f/ in /fʌn/ are linguistically identical means abstracting away from the physical pattern because the two /f/s are not perfectly identical sounds; how we say them is influenced by the following vowels. (Miller, 1990, has a succinct and readable introduction to these two classic problems of speech science, phoneme segmentation and phoneme invariance.)

The children in the experiments reported in Chapter 3 easily learned to read training words like *fat* and *bat* but almost uniformly failed to transfer to words like *fun* and *bun*. Apparently, therefore, one or more of the three components required for decoding—letter knowledge, phoneme segmentation, and phoneme invariance—was not in place. To find out which, we taught these components in an incremental fashion along with the training words to locate the point at which children successfully complete the transfer task. This and other small-scale experiments are described in the next section. After that, we will see what those experiments taught us, if anything, about how to promote acquisition of the alphabetic principle in the classroom.

DATA I: SMALL-SCALE EXPERIMENTS

Incremental instruction in phonemic awareness. The progression implemented in the first experiment is outlined in Table 4.1. It is reported in detail as Experiment 2 in Byrne and Fielding-Barnsley (1989), and involved 12 preschoolers. In *Stage 1*, we introduced the children to a frog puppet who "talked funny, in little bits". He said "m...at" instead of "mat." After several demonstrations, the children were encouraged do the same by operating the frog. Some could do this readily enough (our criterion was being able to do it three times in succession), and some could only do it immediately after hearing the segmented word spoken by the experimenter. Using the same method, we worked our way through all of the words to be used in this experiment (*sat*, the other word to be used in the training phase, followed by the 8 words which comprised the transfer items, like *sow* and *mow*). The children fell into two clear groups, 8 who could segment the next word without hearing it modelled by the experimenter and 4 who could only imitate. In *Stage 2*, we taught all children to read the training items *mat* and *sat* in the usual way (and with the usual success), and in *Stage 3* tested for transfer to *sow*, etc. To our disappointment, none of the 12 reached our transfer criterion of 7/8, and the mean score, at 3.9, was obviously not above the chance value of 1. The 8 children who could segment the words actually scored a mere 3.5 on transfer. So knowing how to divide words into initial phoneme and rime did not help children acquire the alphabetic principle once they had learned to read the very same words that they had learned to segment.

In *Stage 4* we continued to increment the children's understanding of the components necessary for successful transfer by telling them about phoneme identity. We did this by drawing their attention to the fact that "milk", "mouth", "Martin", etc. all began with /m/, and that they contrasted with "sandwich", "silly", "Sally", etc., all of which began with /s/. We provided many examples of /m/ and /s/ words, coupled with explicit advice about their initial identities. To assess whether our instruction had been successful, we pointed out that "mat" started with /m/ as well, requesting the children to say /m/. We then asked them whether it was "mum" or "sum" that started the same as "mat", and whether it was "mow" or "sow" that started like "sat". We continued in this vein, checking for their understanding of phoneme identity with exactly the words that were used to train segmentation and that were the stimuli for the word learning and transfer tests. Thus we could be sure that children who reached our criterion of success, which was 6 out of 8 test questions answered correctly, grasped the idea of phoneme identity in a way that was directly relevant to our test of their understanding of the alphabetic principle. The training went on over two sessions, on separate days.

As it turned out, teaching phoneme identity proved a little more difficult than segmentation in that only 5 of the 12 children reached criterion. Four of those children had also performed well on segmentation, so they at least knew that /m/ and /s/ were discrete constituents of words and that the /m/s and /s/s in the training and transfer words were identical. So we might hope that these 4 at least would succeed at transfer. We made sure that all 12 children could still

TABLE 4.1
Structure of incremental training experiment

Stage	Activity
1.	Phoneme segmentation training, using "sat" and "mat"
2.	Learning to read *sat* and *mat*
3.	Transfer test: *sow* = "sow or mow"?
4.	Phoneme identity training, using /s/ and /m/
5.	Transfer test, as in stage 3
6.	Letter training, using *s* and *m*
7.	Transfer test, as in stage 3

read *sat* and *mat* and then, in *Stage 5*, re-administered the transfer test (does *sat* say "sow" or "mow", etc). But again we were disappointed. Not a single child passed. The mean was just 3.3. Phonemic awareness combined with a memorised word family did not provide a sufficiently firm basis for discovering the alphabetic principle.

Stage 6 was a simple routine to teach the sounds of the letters *m* and *s*, something that proved quite straightforward. All 12 children rapidly learned to say the correct sound when shown each letter.

The seventh and final stage was a repeat of the transfer test. And now at last we had some successes. Six children scored 7 or 8 out of 8, reliable transfer and reliable evidence of the alphabetic principle. Which children? The 4 who had passed both aspects of phonemic awareness and 2 others who had passed one aspect. No child who failed to benefit from segmentation or identity training succeeded at transfer. Remember that all 12 children were now secure in their letter-phoneme knowledge, so that by itself is not sufficient to support the emergence of the alphabetic principle. Remember, too, that 4 of the children had been secure in their phonemic awareness at *Stage 5*, before the letters were taught explicitly, but had failed to pass the transfer test. So phonemic awareness by itself is not sufficient to support the emergence of the alphabetic principle. Apparently letter knowledge and phonemic awareness are needed in combination, or so these experiments indicate.

So did the next experiment in Byrne and Fielding-Barnsley (1989). It used a between-subject design, with three groups of preschoolers. One group constituted a replication of the previous study in that its children received training in both aspects of phonemic awareness, segmentation and identity. Each of the other two groups was only taught one of these skills. All children were taught the words *sat* and *mat*. They were also given the same transfer tests on two occasions, once after the group-appropriate phonemic awareness instruction and once following explicit letter-sound instruction. The results confirm the previous conclusions in two ways: First, none of the groups succeeded at transfer on the occasion of the first test, that is after phonemic awareness instruction but before letter-sound instruction. Second, only children in the group that received both segmentation and identity instruction and who had benefited from it had a mean score above chance on the second transfer test (it was a secure 7.6, maximum 8, and all of the children in the group reached criterion). Before preschoolers can decode part-novel print sequences, they apparently need a clear grasp of the phonemic organisation of the speech stream and relevant letter-sound knowledge.

The results vindicate the earlier suggestion that we need to study separately how phonemic awareness is learned and whether it underpins discovery of the alphabetic principle. Clearly, the former does not lead inevitably to the latter. But it appears to be necessary, and so it makes sense to continue to refine our understanding of how best to teach it. Byrne and Fielding-Barnsley (1989, 1990) describe other experiments aimed at achieving this refinement. The articles also report experiments designed to shed more light on children's early mastery of the alphabetic principle, in particular, on how robust it is once it is attained at all. I summarise these experiments in terms of the questions being investigated.

Phoneme segmentation versus phoneme identity. In the experiments described so far, children needed to be taught both to segment words into phonemes and to recognise the identity of phonemes before they showed signs of the alphabetic principle. But the instruction they received could not be described as especially extensive, and it remains an open question whether both need always to be taught. One reason for raising this question is that there is an asymmetry between the two aspects of phonemic awareness. Phoneme identity entails segmentation, but segmentation does not entail identity. If a child understands that "mat" and "mow" begin with the same sound, he or she must have parsed the words sufficiently to make the judgement. This is tantamount to saying that the segmental status of the initial segments has registered. In contrast, breaking "mat" and "mow" into initial segment and rime does not entail noticing the identity of the initial segments, that is, that both words start with the same phoneme. For this reason, phoneme identity appears to offer good prospects as a vehicle for bringing to the child's awareness the alphabetically relevant property of phonemic structure: In a single step, the child can be taught that words are segmental and that the same segment can occur in different words.

To this end, we again instructed two groups of preschoolers separately in phoneme identity and phoneme segmentation, but this time instituted a more extensive teaching programme extending over four days. We used four phonemes instead of two, had a larger number of exemplars (six) for each phoneme, and included instruction in final as well as initial segments (e.g., that "bus", "dress", and "octopus" ended with /s/, or how to say "bu...s", "dre...ss", etc.). For each group, we tested how well the children achieved the relevant kind of phonemic awareness, identity or segmentation, using test words that differed from the training items. In the segmentation group, we also tested for phoneme identity at the end of training, acting on a hunch that extensive repetition of a small group of sounds might draw identity to the children's attention. Following phonemic awareness training, we taught the children to read *sat* and *mat*, and tested for transfer in the usual way.

We noticed, first, that phoneme identity was a more stable construct than phoneme segmentation, once grasped. Children who did well on one phoneme had a strong tendency to do well on all the others. For segmentation, this was not the case; children could manage the segmentation of some sounds well but perform poorly on others. More importantly, we found a very close relation between identity and decoding (as assessed by the transfer test, does *mow* say "mow" or "sow"?), but a weaker one between segmentation and decoding. In the Identity group, the nine children who reached our passing criterion on the transfer test (7 of 8 items correct) were precisely the nine children who scored highest on the phoneme identity test at the end of training. In the Segmentation group, five children passed on the transfer (decoding) test, and these were not the five most successful segmenters (their ranks ranged from second to eleventh). Most interesting of all, we found that among the children taught segmentation, the correlation between phoneme identity performance (which you will recall we also measured) was significant at .49 but the correlation between segmentation score and decoding was nonsignificant at .20. In fact, it was *only* children who succeeded in grasping the idea of identity as a by-product of their segmentation lessons who reached criterion on the transfer test. So it seems that some of the good effects of segmentation instruction are mediated by phoneme identity, and that identity is the more reliable way to give the child useable insights into phonemic structure.

Phonetic properties and phonemic awareness training. Are some phonemes better vehicles for teaching phoneme identity than others? We know already that children in our population learn the names and sounds of some letters, particularly /s/ and /m/, earlier than others. Note that both /s/ and /m/ can be prolonged in pronunciation ("ssssssat", "mmmmmat"). In contrast, you cannot hold a /b/ or a /d/ in the same way. Nor can you say a /b/ or a /d/ without attaching a vowel, as in "buh" or "duh". Perhaps the phonetic class makes a difference to how easily children can learn about sounds. To check on this, in Experiments 4–6 of Byrne and Fielding-Barnsley (1990) we compared the teachability of a variety of phonemes with a benchmark, /s/, the best-known letter name and sound in our sample of children. We found, indeed, that stops, in our selection /t/, /d/, /k/, and /g/, as a group were more difficult as target phonemes in identity instruction than /s/. In fact, a more general comparison of three continuants, /s/, /ʃ/ and /m/, and these four stops, collected from a variety of experiments in this series, confirmed that continuants provide a better point of entry for teaching phoneme identity than do stops. The vowel /i/ presented a target as accessible as

/s/. Finally, we found that it was not especially difficult to teach about /s/ when it was part of a consonant cluster, as in "star", "spade", "nest", and "tusk". Treiman (1985) noted that clusters do present children with difficulties of analysis. Whether our relative success in teaching phoneme identity using a consonant that was part of a cluster was due to the choice of /s/, which some linguists think may retain its independent status even in clusters (Kaye, 1989), or to our teaching methods, is not clear.

The robustness of the alphabetic principle: Phoneme position. Once children have achieved a degree of phonemic awareness, as indicated by their ability to judge reliably that words can start with the same phoneme, and once they know how these phonemes are represented by letters, they show the beginnings of decoding by being able to decide which of two spoken words a novel printed word stands for. But so far we have only shown that this kind of decoding can occur within the confines of the specific instruction they have been given. Can children decode in contexts divorced from the instruction they received? One type of change is in the position of the critical item in the word. In Experiment 5 of Byrne and Fielding-Barnsley (1989), we asked children who had been through our teaching procedure for phoneme identity and letter-phoneme relations and who had been successful in the transfer task (does *mow* say "sow" or "mow"?) to decode the ends of words. We challenged them with questions like "does *plum* say 'plum' or 'plus'?, does *bus* say 'bum' or 'bus'?"). The majority of the children, 8 of 11 in the experiment, could do this task reliably. This result is encouraging in that it indicates a degree of robustness in newly acquired alphabetic insight. But the fact that some of the children could not decode in a position different from the one in which they had been taught also suggests that for some the alphabetic principle may be more fragile. They may need more extensive instruction, including help to realise that the principle is position-independent, before they have broadly useable decoding skills.

We extended this experiment with new groups of children (Byrne & Fielding-Barnsley, 1990, Experiment 3). Some were taught phoneme identity for word beginnings only, some for endings only, and some in both positions. They were all then taught to read *sat* and *mat* and tested for transfer to *sow, mow*, etc. in the usual way. In addition, and on a separate day, they were taught to read *bus* and *bum* and tested for transfer to *plum, plus*, etc. (that is, to words with the critical letters at the end). We were interested to know if transfer was affected by whether identity training was word-initial, word-final, or occurred in both positions. It was not. Children who were only taught in one position, either initial or final, were as successful in the transfer task in the other position (final or initial) as were the children trained in the other position. Children taught phoneme identity in both positions were no better at transfer in either position than the children taught in just initial position or the children taught in just final position. Again, we had evidence of the robustness of the alphabetic principle, once acquired.

In many teaching programmes, the focus is on sounds at the beginning of words (*a* for *apple*, *b* for *banana*). Is this a wise policy? Our data sanction it in part. For most children, transfer performance, our measure of decoding for preschoolers, was independent of the position in which phoneme awareness had been trained and in which the critical letters had occurred in the word-training set. But for some children position still mattered. So the properly conservative policy might be to teach phoneme structure in a variety of word positions; it can hardly hurt children who do not need it, and can only help children who do.

The robustness of the alphabetic principle: New letters.   In Experiments 1 and 2 of Byrne and Fielding-Barnsley (1990), the ones in which we trained phoneme identity and phoneme segmentation separately, we checked for whether successful transfer performance could be generated for letters not part of the experiments' instructional regimens. We did this by teaching two new words, *fat* and *bat*, as the last stage of the experiment, along with the sounds of their distinctive letters *f* and *b*. The phonemes /f/ and /b/ had not been used in the earlier identity and segmentation phases. Recall that in none of our experiments so far had children who had been taught words and their distinctive letters shown successful transfer. All had needed phonemic awareness training for the critical sounds as well.

On this occasion, however, transfer (does *fun* say "fun" or "bun"? etc.) was above chance among the children who had succeeded in transfer with *s* and *m* (which were included among the phonemes selected for awareness instruction). For some children, therefore, alphabetic insight can extend beyond the boundaries of the phonemic sites in which it was first generated. But not for all children, it seems. Some who had passed on *s* and *m* failed with *f* and *b*. This is further evidence that instruction may need to cover wider ground for some children, and again raises a point of educational strategy; given that some children need extensive instruction, assuming that all do may be the safest course.

Summary.   These small-scale experiments have provided a positive answer to the first of our questions: Can children be made aware of the phonemic structure of the speech stream? The answer is yes. To the second question—Does this awareness enable them to grasp the alphabetic principle as they learn to read words?—the answer is a qualified yes. It is qualified in that phonemic awareness needs to be bolstered by specific letter-phoneme knowledge. When both aspects of knowledge are in place, most preschool children can resolve the pronunciation of a novel printed word when the decision space is restricted. They show the beginnings of decoding. Armed with these observations, we set out to develop and test a teaching programme focused on phoneme identity. That research is described next.

DATA II: CLASSROOM RESEARCH

Design of the teaching programme.   The focus in the programme, which is entitled *Sound Foundations* (Byrne & Fielding-Barnsley, 1991b), is on phoneme identity, a decision based on the research just described. Nine phonemes receive most attention, the fricative continuants /s/ and /ʃ/, the nasal /m/, the lateral /l/, the stops /p/, /t/, and /g/, and the vowels /æ/ and /ɛ/. Five of these phonemes are voiced, four are unvoiced. Thus the major phonetic classes are represented. For each of the seven consonants there are two large colored posters, one containing many items beginning with that consonant (e.g., sun, sea, sailor, sand) and one containing items ending with that consonant (e.g., bus, horse, hippopotamus, octopus). The posters for the vowels are word-initial only (e.g., ambulance, axe, astronaut, anchor). English has virtually no words ending with these particular vowels. About 60% of the items in each poster start or end with the target phoneme. Figure 4.1 shows two of the posters in outline form. The artwork for the posters and for the remainder of the kit was produced by Hilary Pollock.

For these nine phonemes, as well as for the other phonemes represented by the remaining letters of the alphabet (*b, c, d, f*, etc.), there are worksheets with outline drawings of characters and objects whose names begin with the phoneme. On each worksheet, about half of the items begin with the critical sound, and the child's task is to locate and colour the target items. For the nine main phonemes, worksheets for ending sounds were also created.

There are two card games, based on four of the phonemes, /s/, /t/, /p/, /l/. One is a form of dominoes, with two pictured objects on each card. The child's task is to join cards sharing beginning sounds (or ending sounds, in a second version). The other game has one picture per card, and is a form of Snap in which children win by quickly noticing that a card placed on top of another has a picture which starts the same as the previous card. There is also an audio tape, with stories and poems that repetitively emphasise the nine central phonemes.

FIG. 4.1.   Outline drawings of two posters from *Sound Foundations:* (A) beginning /m/; and (B) ending /g/. (Copyright © 1991 Peter Leyden Educational Publishers. Adapted with permission.)

Evaluation: Preschool phase.   To evaluate the programme, we compared an instructed experimental group with a control group given a kind of placebo instruction (see later). The first phase of the evaluation is reported in detail in Byrne and Fielding-Barnsley (1991a). For the trial, we used just six of the nine key phonemes, /s/, /m/, /p/, /t/, /l/, and /æ/. We opted for teaching the children in small groups, ranging from four to six children. They had a half-hour session each week, concentrating on one phoneme in one position per week. We began with /s/, mindful of our earlier research that showed that continuants may provide better material for teaching phoneme identity than stops. The final session was devoted to the card games. This functioned as a revision and reinforcement lesson, and for it to work as such the children need to have grasped the idea of phoneme identity for at least four phonemes used in the games. In all, there were 12 sessions, 10 for the five consonants in beginning and end positions, 1 for the vowel, and the games session. Thus, for the children in the experimental group there was around six hours' exposure to the idea of phoneme identity.

The lessons themselves began with the teacher, Ruth Fielding-Barnsley, reciting the story and poem, and drawing attention to the sound and how it is made by the mouth. The poster was introduced, and each child in turn was invited to find something beginning with the day's sound in its position. Liberal feedback was provided, with children given opportunities to try again if they failed to find an object. Further chances to learn the concept of phoneme identity came with the worksheets, which were provided for each child. Because our aim was to ensure that as many children as possible left the programme understanding what we were trying to teach, and because the small group format allowed close monitoring of individual children, special attention was directed to those children struggling with the idea of phoneme identity. It was explained anew as necessary. Throughout the first 11 lessons, the relevant letter was displayed, and the children were told that it "said" the phoneme.

We had 64 children in the experimental group, 35 boys and 29 girls. Their average age at the beginning was 55 months. We also established a control group, 62 children in all (we began with 64 but 2 left the region during the first year), 34 boys and 28 girls, average age also 55 months. The major difference in the way these children were treated was that instead of being taught to classify the objects in the posters and games by common phoneme, they were taught to classify along semantic and physical lines. They might be asked to find red things, or edible things, or the animals. At the start of each of their 12 sessions, they were read regular instead of alliterative stories and poems. But they had the same amount of time with the same teacher being exposed to the same material as the experimental group children, and were also in groups of four to six. This kind of "semantic" control group was originally used by Bradley and Bryant (1983) in their pioneering training study. As a control, it is superior to using a comparison group that receives no teaching at all. However, in our case, we need to acknowledge that the teacher was not naive to the purpose of the study, or to the hypothesis that training in phoneme identity would be beneficial to the children. This is a limitation on the study—it is better to have "blind" researchers collecting data—but the good fit of our results to other people's, described later in the chapter, gives us confidence that this factor did not unduly influence the teaching or the children.

Our pre- and posttests reflected the questions we were addressing. They were (1) can phonemic awareness be taught to preschoolers, this time using a group approach and a commercially available instructional programme, and (2) if so, does it promote acquisition of the alphabetic principle as indicated by successful decoding performance. So we assessed the children's grasp of phoneme identity before teaching began and again afterwards, using the test described in Chapter 3 (see Fig. 3.1). Recall that the items in the tests each had a target picture, like a lamp, and three test pictures, like a heart, a lock, and a shoe. We assessed both beginning and ending sounds, using four phonemes that would be part of the instruction, /s/, /m/, /p/, /l/, and four that would not, /f/, /n/, /b/, /k/. At pretest, we also checked on how well the children could recognise rhyme (which words rhymes with *cat; hat, clock, bed*?, with pictures of the items). We measured vocabulary, with the Peabody Picture Vocabulary Test (PPVT), and tested the children's knowledge of print conventions, using Clay's (1975) Concepts About Print test. This test checks children's understanding of things like the difference between print and drawing, where the front of the book is, and the difference between upper and lower case letters. We also assessed the children's recognition of letter names and letter sounds, and asked them to name six common signs, like *Stop, McDonalds*, and *Taxi*.

The experimental and control groups were well-matched on all of the pretest variables (see Table 1 in Byrne and Fielding-Barnsley (1991a), and it turned out that we had a representative sample of children in both groups in terms of verbal intelligence. The means of both groups on the PPVT were close to population value of 100, and the standard deviations were close to 15, also the population value.

The posttests included (1) a repeat of the four subscales of the phoneme identity test (beginning and end sounds, both taught and untaught), (2) a forced-choice decoding test in which a word constructed from the trained sounds, like *sat*, was shown and the children were invited to choose between "sat" and "mat" as its pronunciation, and (3) knowledge of the sound of the letters used in the decoding test, namely, *s, m, p, t, l, a.*

Performance on each of the four 12-item phoneme identity pre- and posttests is shown in Fig. 4.2. Two trends are obvious: First, improvement was much more substantial for the experimental group than the control group. Second, the experimental group improved as much on the untrained items as on the trained ones (the change in untrained phonemes was not significantly lower than the change in trained phonemes).

The experimental group's data show that phonemic awareness can be taught to preschool children. In fact, 61 of the 64 children in that group could be classed as having achieved phonemic awareness, using a reasonably stringent criterion of 67% correct in a three-alternative test (chance = 33%). Some "spontaneous" gains occurred among control children over the four months between pre- and posttesting, as we might expect from children attending preschool.

It is equally clear that once preschoolers have the idea of phoneme identity for some sounds, it generalises unaided to other sounds. This aspect of the data backs up observations of generalisability made already in the small-scale experiments described earlier. It is

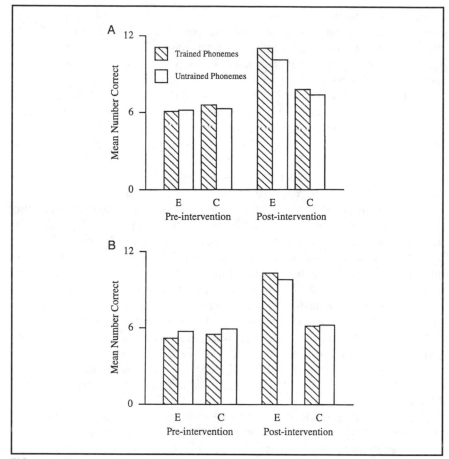

FIG. 4.2.   Mean scores of experimental (E) and control (C) groups on phoneme identity for trained and untrained phonemes, pre- and post-intervention: (A) initial phonemes; (B) final phonemes.

encouraging news in that it implies that in teaching phonemic awareness we do not have to work our way laboriously through all the sounds of the language. It is an example of the child's contribution to the learning task, knowledge that is inferred from limited evidence.

So far so good, but what of the second question, the one about discovery of the alphabetic principle? That, too, was answered in the positive. The mean of the experimental group on the 12-item decoding test was 8.1, significantly above the guessing score of 6. In contrast, the control group only managed to score 6.1, not above the guessing value.

The decoding data can be subject to a more telling analysis. Recall that in the small-scale experiments only children who had achieved some degree of phonemic awareness and had learned letter-phoneme relations were successful in the transfer task, that is in decoding. We checked for a similar pattern in these data by classifying children into those who passed and those who failed on each of three measures—phoneme identity, letter knowledge, and decoding. For decoding, our dependent variable, we set the pass criterion at 9/12. Letter knowledge was based on the six critical letters, and to pass the child needed to be able to give us the sound of four of the five consonants. The vowel a was disregarded because it did not serve a discriminating function; it was present in all of the test words. Knowing four consonants would permit perfect performance in a forced-choice test. The criterion for phoneme identity was set at 67%, which equalled 32 out of 48 (chance = 16).

These data are presented as a set of contingencies in Table 4.2. On the hypothesis that children need to be phonemically aware and secure in their letter knowledge, there should be no entries in the D+ columns except under the L+I+ heading. That is, only children who pass both tests, phoneme identity and letter knowledge, should also pass decoding. That is largely the case, though three children violate the prediction. It happens, however, that each of the three may be less of a threat to the hypothesis than it seems on the surface. The control group child who failed identity but passed decoding in fact had done well with initial phonemes but failed to reach criterion on final phonemes. In the decoding test, half of the items had the choice point at the beginning (*sat* versus *mat*, for example) and half had it at the end (*pal* versus *pat*). Being secure on initial phonemes would increase the chances of passing the decoding test. One of the two experimental group children who failed the letter test but passed decoding was a Japanese girl who looked for r instead of l but knew three of the other four letter sounds. This too would give her a firm base for decoding in our forced-choice test. The other child in this category knew the names but not the sounds of the letters (generating the sounds was our measure of letter knowledge).

TABLE 4.2
Numbers of children passing and failing on decoding, letter knowledge, and phoneme identity

	$L+I+$	$L+I-$	$L-I+$	$L-I-$
D+	36	1	2	0
D–	9	10	33	34

Note: + = Pass, – = Fail, D = Decoding, L = Letter Knowledge, I = Phoneme Identity

Names are generally a useful guide to the role of particular letters in the pronunciation of words, as Ehri and Wilce (1985) have shown. So the hypothesis that phonemic awareness and letter knowledge are needed in combination to support the early stages of decoding appears relatively intact from this contingency analysis.

Note that there was a sizeable minority of children who had both of the building blocks of decoding but who still failed on the decoding test, 9 out of 45. These 9 included 6 from the experimental group. This means that phonemic awareness and letter knowledge are not sufficient for decoding, even though they appear to be necessary. It is obviously important to identify the factors that are needed to supplement phonemic awareness and letter knowledge to ensure the emergence of decoding skill.

One particularly telling aspect of the data in Table 4.2 is the decoding performance of the children, 10 in all, who knew the relevant letter sounds but who had failed on the phoneme identity test. They failed on decoding. Even though they knew that *s* made the sound /s/, they could not decide that *sat* said "sat" rather than "mat". It appears that letter-sound knowledge unaccompanied by insights into the phonemic structure of speech is of little use in decoding novel printed words. We had shown that to be the case in one of our small-scale experiments as well (see earlier).

We can analyse the influences on decoding performance as continuous rather than categorical data in a multiple regression. If we enter letter knowledge as the first step in an analysis predicting decoding score, we account for 43% of the variance. Adding the children's scores on the posttest of phoneme identity increases the variance explained by a highly significant 11%, to 54%. So letter knowledge and phonemic awareness make separate and substantial contributions to children's ability to make sense of novel print sequences. But a reasonable amount of variance remains unexplained. As we saw from the contingency data in Table 4.2, most of it is in the form of children being secure in these two building blocks of decoding but not being able to decode. We will see that this is repeated in later school years, and in different kinds of data.

Predicting preschool phonemic awareness.   Given the importance of phonemic awareness to emerging decoding skill, we should try to discover what characteristics of children best predict its own emergence. We will examine this question in more detail in the next chapter, but some remarks are appropriate here.

With the present data set we already know that our experimental intervention was effective, and this was confirmed in a regression analysis where we find that group membership accounts for 47% of the variance in the posttest phoneme identity scores of the children. Do any of our other variables measured prior to the intervention phase predict how well a child will fare at posttest? Naturally, the pretest score on the same variable, phoneme identity, would be expected to have a role, and when we add it to the regression equation 65% of the variance is accounted for. Neither of these results is surprising or informative, the first because it is just another way of expressing the treatment effect, and the second because it would be surprising if things did not turn out that way. What is more interesting is whether any less obvious variables predict post-treatment phonemic awareness. One that does is pretest rhyme score. It adds another, significant 4% to the variance accounted for, now at 69%. This is in line with an observation made by Bryant, Bradley, Maclean, and Crossland (1989) that measures of rhyme knowledge taken prior to school predict reading performance in school several years later. It may be that rhyming ability paves the way for children to become aware of smaller, phonemic units in language by drawing their attention to the facts of phonology in a general way. Rimes are more visible in the speech stream than phonemes, as we have seen, and rhyme awareness may be the precursor for full phonemic awareness for some children.

Another variable that predicts phoneme identity score is our measure of verbal intelligence, the PPVT. The correlation between it and the posttest was a significant .21. However, all of that influence can be explained by the correlation between verbal IQ and pre-existing levels of phonemic awareness, that is, between the PPVT and pretest phoneme identity, measured at .48. In a regression analysis, the pretest identity score alone accounts for 17% of the variance in posttest score, and the PPVT adds nothing at all to the variance explained. This situation holds for both the experimental group and the control group analysed separately: The amounts of variance in posttest phoneme identity accounted for by pretest phoneme identity were 23% and 51% in the two groups, respectively, with the PPVT explaining no further variance in either case. (The lower value for the experimental group reflects the fact that almost all of its children achieved high scores at posttest, restricting the total variance.)

The total pattern of results means that verbal IQ does relate to levels of phonemic awareness quite early in a child's development, but that it does not seem to play a continuing role in the face of intensive instruction in phonemic awareness (experimental group data, showing both high levels of phoneme identity and no further effect of IQ) and in the face of natural opportunities to advance in phonemic awareness (control group data). This is good news in that children of varying verbal IQ levels could be expected to respond equally well to appropriately tailored instruction in the foundations of literacy, and even to unstructured information available in their social contexts.

There is also a kind of good news in the data on how pre-existing levels of print knowledge affects post-intervention levels of phonemic awareness. For the group as a whole, neither Concepts About Print nor letter-sound knowledge added significantly to variance explained, when entered after pre-intervention phoneme identity and rhyme. Letter-name knowledge did add a little, but only 1%. When we analyse the experimental group data alone, even this small effect disappears (although the effects of pretest phoneme identity and rhyme remain strong at 20% and 8% of variance accounted for in posttest phoneme identity, respectively). Thus, our instruction overcame the apparent disadvantages of low levels of print knowledge and the social conditions that foster it. We also know that print knowledge, in the form of letter names, does remain involved in what we could call the *natural growth* of phonemic awareness. When we analyse the control group data alone, we find that letter names, assessed at the beginning of the study, accounts for 5% of the variance in phoneme identity measured four to five months later, at the end of the intervention phase. (Concepts About Print and letter-*sound* knowledge did not explain significant levels of variance after pretest phoneme identity and rhyme were taken into account.) So in the absence of intensive instruction in phonemic structure, children who start out with advanced levels of letter awareness tend to go further ahead. Of course we cannot say that letter knowledge causes these further advancements in phonemic awareness, or vice versa. More likely, home environments that promote one also promote the other. The important point is the contrast with the experimental group, and its implication that good teaching can bring almost all children up to high levels in this important foundation of literacy development, even if they start with low levels of familiarity with the letters of the alphabet.

Review, and related studies.   Let us stand back and review what we have demonstrated. We have shown that preschool children can be taught that words share sounds and that when this insight is combined with knowledge of the sounds of relevant letters children show signs of emerging decoding skill. Our index of this skill was a forced choice between two pronunciations for a printed word made up of phonemes and letters to which the children had been exposed in the experimental intervention. We have shown that the combination of foundation insights and knowledge does not guarantee the emergence of decoding, so some other factors must be at work. We showed that almost all of the children given the experimental instruction benefited from it, and that this benefit was independent of verbal IQ as measured by a vocabulary test. In both taught and untaught children, pre-existing levels of rhyme awareness influenced the final outcome on the phoneme identity test, but it was only in the untaught children that there was any sign that knowledge of print, in the form of letter name familiarity, related to phoneme identity.

Let us also consider what we have not demonstrated. We have not shown that any of the children can read, in the sense of being able to take a string of letters and decode them. Our test has always been one in which the response space was very restricted, and the alternatives always provided. We have every reason to suspect that our four-year-olds could do no more with written words. So we have a long way to go before we can claim that preschool instruction in phoneme structure has a subsequent effect on reading skill, either on learning to read words where the teacher provides the pronunciation or on working out the pronunciation independently. We will consider evidence on these questions shortly, as we follow the children into school. But we do have reason to hope that our intervention will be beneficial because other groups' research has shown that the things we taught do influence variables that are more ecologically valid than our forced-choice decoding task.

One research programme that did this was a pioneering study by Bradley and Bryant (1983). These authors selected preschool children with low levels of phonological awareness and instituted phonemic awareness training similar to ours over a two-year period. Children were taught to classify the names of objects by their starting sounds. One group was additionally given intensive instruction in the letters of the alphabet. Another, a control group, was taught to classify the objects in the teaching material along semantic and formal grounds, just as we did with our control children. Yet another group received no intervention of any sort. When reading and spelling performance were checked at the end of the project using standardised tests, it was the children given both phonemic awareness and letter training that stood out from the rest. This result nicely mirrors our finding that it is the combination of phonemic awareness and letter knowledge that sets the scene for literacy development. It is encouraging to see that this remains so when development is assessed with regular reading and spelling tests.

A second finding that encourages us in thinking that we are on the right track is that word learning can benefit from letter knowledge even before children can read novel written words. Ehri and Wilce (1985) found that very young children could exploit letter knowledge in learning new words. Their subjects were better able to learn *MSK* for *mask* and *LFT* for *elephant* than visually distinctive letter groups like *uHE* for *mask*. The results showed that letter names, like "el", can form anchor points for learning new words when the names form part of the words' pronunciations, as in "elephant". Rack, Hulme, Snowling, and Wightman (1994) extended this result by showing that kindergarten children learned truncated words like these better even when the critical "phonetic cue", as Ehri and Wilce called it, was similar rather than identical to the relevant phoneme. Thus, their subjects more easily learned *bzn* than *bfn* for *basin*. The phonemes /s/ and /z/ are similar in that they share the salient property of place of articulation; /s/ and /t/ do not, and are therefore less similar. Importantly, the results held up even when the analysis was restricted to children who could not read simple strings of letters like *hin* and *sted*. Although Rack et al. did not assess letter knowledge independently, we can only presume that their subjects knew their letters. So, although letter knowledge alone does not support decoding as defined by the ability to read novel letter strings from scratch (see next paragraph), it certainly helps children learn to remember new words whose pronunciations they are told.

We do not know from the Ehri and Wilce (1985) and Rack et al. (1994) studies what role, if any, phonemic awareness played in their subjects' processing. None, perhaps. After all, the Rack et al. manipulation depended on phonetic similarity (/s/ and /z/, for instance), and it is not at all clear than kindergarten children would judge phonemes to be more or less "similar" in an appropriate test.[1] But recall that in our research just described, children who knew relevant letter-sound correspondences but lacked phonemic awareness could not decode (could not decide that *sat* said "sat" rather than "mat"—see Table 4.2). Conceivably, therefore, learning the pronunciation of words, which is assisted by knowing letter sounds, represents a different skill from making sense of new words, which is not assisted by letter-sound knowledge in the absence of phonemic awareness. The degree to which memorising the pronunciation of printed words and mastering decoding are related, and the important question of these skills' relative reliance on phonemic awareness, deserve more research.

In sum, our study is not alone in pointing to the importance of phonemic awareness, letter knowledge, and their combination in promoting literacy development in the early stages. The studies reviewed complement our research with the use of different, and arguably more ecologically valid, measures of reading and spelling progress.

We now turn to the follow-up studies of our preschoolers. A central feature of this research is the use of nonword reading as a measure of literacy growth, which allows us further opportunities to study conditions that foster the important skill of independent decoding of novel print sequences.

Evaluation: Kindergarten.   The first follow-up data were collected a year after the completion of the preschool intervention, and are reported in Byrne and Fielding-Barnsley (1993a). The number of children remaining in the study at the end of kindergarten (the first school year in Australia) was 119, 63 from the experimental groups and 56 from the control group. The children had dispersed into 19 separate classes in 10 different schools. We used the Word Identification subtest from the Woodcock Reading Mastery Test, Revised, Form G (Woodcock, 1987) to measure real word reading. In it, children have to provide the pronunciation for words, starting with simple ones like *is* and *and* , then moving on to more complex ones like *play* and *milk*, until they make six consecutive errors. To measure the children's ability to deal with novel print sequences, we developed a forced-choice test in which the child heard a nonword, like "ap", and was required to select its written version from three alternatives. These alternatives were constructed so that the right answer could not be given on the basis of a single known letter. For example, the alternatives for "ap" were *ap, ep*, and *aj*. Spelling was tested using 10 real words, like *man, dog, said*, and *blue*, and 4 nonwords, like *sut* and *yilt*. We also retested the children on phoneme identity and alphabet knowledge.

The experimental group did significantly better on the test of nonword decoding, confirming that group's advantage, originally observed in preschool, in dealing with novel written forms. The data are presented graphically in Fig. 4.3. The experimental children bunch up at the high end of the score range, with close to half at or near ceiling. In contrast, the control group contains some children who performed at ceiling, with the rest spread throughout the range.

However, the newly tested skills of real word reading and spelling did not show advantages for the experimental group. The experimental group achieved a Woodcock Word Identification scaled score of 110.6, the control group one of 108.6, not close to a significant difference. At first sight, therefore, it seems as if the advantage for the phonemically aware children only extended to nonword reading. That in itself would not be a bad thing. We might expect that if nonword reading is a proxy for being able to independently decipher novel real words then children so equipped should be well placed to advance in literacy during the early school years.

However, a different analysis was more encouraging for the hypothesis that early insights into phonemic structure supports literacy development in a broad way. Recall that a few children (3 out of 64) from the experimental group had not reached our pass criterion for phoneme identity at the preschool posttest. Analogously, some of the children from the control group, 20 out of 62, had reached that criterion (16 of these

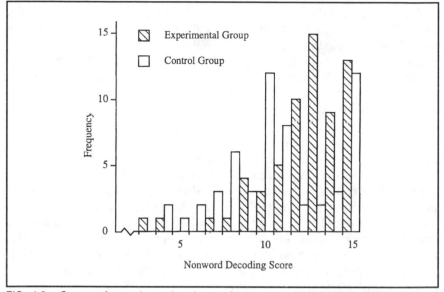

FIG. 4.3.   Scores of experimental and control groups on 15-item kindergarten nonword decoding test.

remained in the area for the follow-up study). Some of these children would have been numbered among those who had high levels of phonemic awareness prior to the intervention phase, the 29% of children mentioned in the previous chapter. Some would have discovered phoneme identity for themselves during the period of the experiment, perhaps stimulated by preschool experiences, or by television, or by family word games, or ... In any case, we set no store by *how* children come to understand the principle of phoneme identity, just by the fact that they do. Thus, we reclassified the children into those who had reached criterion on phoneme identity at the end of preschool and those who had not. Using this split, there were significant differences a year after the preschool intervention in all three measures of literacy growth—real word identification, nonword decoding, and spelling—in favour of the phonemically aware children. The mean scores are in Table 4.3.

In the preschool data we showed that alphabet knowledge and phonemic awareness made independent contributions to our measure of emerging literacy, the forced-choice decoding test. We looked for similar evidence in the kindergarten results, using our re-assessments of alphabet knowledge and phoneme identity. One problem with the latter variable was that by now most of the children had reached ceiling, particularly on initial phonemes, presumably because of teaching that focused on beginning sounds of words. However, the mean score for final

TABLE 4.3
Mean kindergarten scores on three literacy measures achieved by children classified as passing and failing on phoneme identity in preschool

Group	Measure		
	Woodcock Word Identification [a]	Decoding [b]	Spelling [c]
Passing children	112.7	12.4	59.1
Failing children	104.4	10.0	49.3

Note: All differences statistically significant.
[a] = Scaled score, [b] Maximum = 15, [c] Maximum = 84.
Copyright © 1993 American Psychological Association. Adapted with permission.

phonemes was somewhat below ceiling, especially for control children. It looks as if final phoneme identity is a kind of "acid test" of phonemic awareness in kindergarten children. In any case, that gave us some variance to include in regression analyses. Accordingly, we selected each of the three literacy measures in turn as the dependent variable, and entered alphabet knowledge and word-final phoneme identity scores in that order as predictors. The results are shown in Table 4.4.

In each case, knowing the letters of the alphabet accounted for substantial amounts of variance, and in each case phonemic awareness added to the variance explained to a significant degree. So again we have evidence for the notion that the twin foundations of literacy development are an appreciation of the phonemic organisation of speech and specific knowledge of the letters representing the phonemes.[2]

TABLE 4.4
Prediction of three kindergarten literacy measures from alphabet knowledge and phoneme identity

	Measure		
	Woodcock Word Identification R^2 change	Decoding R^2 change	Spelling R^2 change
Step 1 Alphabet knowledge	0.42	0.24	0.49
Step 2 Phoneme identity	0.03	0.16	0.07

Note: All values statistically significant.

In sum, the data demonstrate that children who enter kindergarten with advanced levels of phonemic awareness, phoneme identity in particular, prosper in the important skills of word identification, nonword decoding, and spelling. For each of these measures, phonemic awareness and letter knowledge form partially independent foundations.

Evaluation: Grade 1.   In the children's second year at school, Grade 1, we refined the reading and spelling tests by dividing the items into:

1.   real words that follow regular rules at the level of individual letters, like *in, let,* and *hand,*
2.   real words that are irregularly spelled, like one, said, and *right,* and
3.   nonwords like *sut, yent,* and *noxtof.*

On this occasion, the children read the nonwords without the benefit of alternative pronunciations provided by the experimenter, in contrast to preschool and kindergarten. The results of all tests are described in Byrne and Fielding-Barnsley (1995).

The comparison of the experimental and control groups on reading produced a similar situation to kindergarten. The experimental group children scored significantly higher on decoding novel words, the nonword test, but not on either of the real word lists (although the regular words came close, with a p-value in favour of the experimental group of .06). However, when the classification was based on preschool score on the phoneme identity test ("pass" or "fail"), the children who passed were significantly superior on all three lists.

Spelling, however, failed to show significant group differences on either analysis, experimental versus control preschoolers, or those passing versus those failing. The effects of preschool differences in phonemic awareness on spelling seem to have washed out after two years in school. We have no ready explanation for this, except to note that by this stage virtually all children were at ceiling on phoneme identity and alphabet knowledge, which we had also re-assessed in Grade 1. (The means for alphabet knowledge were 24.5 and 24.9 for the experimental and control groups, respectively, and on a new 20-item phoneme identity test the means, in order, were 19.0 and 18.4.) Given the demonstrated dependence on spelling on these foundations, perhaps the highly deliberate task of turning sound into writing only depends on current levels of the basic skills. In contrast, reading is, by Grade 1, an increasingly automated task that still benefits from the overlearning that an early start affords.

Evaluation: Grade 2. The third school year's results are also reported in Byrne and Fielding-Barnsley (1995). We again assessed regular and irregular word reading and nonword reading, and this time included two tests of comprehension. One was reading comprehension, comprising a passage of 160 words and 10 questions based on the passage. The questions were read to the children so as not to confound passage comprehension with question reading ability. The second was a 160-word listening comprehension passage, delivered to the children from a tape recording. Again, there were 10 questions, also read to the children. (In the experiment, the two comprehension tests were alternated between reading and listening modes, so that half the children read Passage A and listened to Passage B, and half had the reverse arrangement.)

For Grade 2 we also introduced a measure of exposure to written language in the form of a test called the *Title Recognition Test*. It was adapted from Cunningham and Stanovich (1990). The test contains the names of real book titles, like *The enormous crocodile* and *Far out, brussel sprout*, along with some plausible-sounding foils like *Katie of Norway* and *Swimming with the sharks*. The children's task is simply to indicate those titles they have heard of. The purpose of the foils is to detect and adjust for false positives.

The data bear some resemblances to the Grade 1 results. In the comparison of the experimental and control groups on isolated word reading, it was only the nonwords that discriminated between the conditions, a highly significant 18% superiority for the experimental group. There was no mean difference between the two groups on the regular and irregular lists. However, on this occasion we assessed separately the children's performance on the five least frequent of the regular words, on the assumption that they would be least likely to be known as sight words and therefore most likely to need decoding in the same way as nonwords. Those words were *hundred, topic, silk, crop*, and *tax*, and as a group they were more poorly read than the other 25 words (82.2% correct versus 93.9%, respectively, averaged across all children). The experimental group was significantly better at reading them than the control group (respective means of 4.4 and 3.9), supporting the general notion that the words that children need to read independently, the ones least frequently encountered, benefit from secure decoding skills.

The second resemblance of the Grade 2 results to the Grade 1 results was with the reclassification of the children into those reaching and those failing to reach criterion on phoneme identity in preschool. This split again produced significant differences in favour of the passing children on the regular and irregular word lists, as well as maintaining the differential on the nonwords. The differences were not very great in numerical terms—28.9 versus 27.8/30 for regular words and 25.1 versus 22.8/30 for irregular words—but the fact they existed at all three years after preschool is testimony to the long-term influence on literacy progress of levels of phonemic awareness prior to the start of formal schooling.

Perhaps the most telling of the Grade 2 results was a modest but significant difference in favour of the experimental group on reading comprehension. We used z-scores for the comprehension tests because it turned out that the two passages were of unequal difficulty. The experimental group's score was +.22, the control group's, −.19. There was no significant difference between the groups on listening comprehension, suggesting that the experimental group's advantage lay in factors specific to reading and not general to language.

The most appropriate framework for considering the interplay between listening and reading is Hoover and Gough's (1990) "simple view" of reading, which holds that reading comprehension is jointly determined by single-word identification and listening comprehension, with the two factors interacting in a multiplicative way. Under this model, if two groups differ on reading comprehension, their relative status on a measure of listening comprehension is crucial for determining whether the reading comprehension difference can be ascribed to word identification processes (decoding). There is no special mystery about a reading comprehension difference if one group is simply better at dealing with language whatever its mode of input (e.g., due to superior vocabulary). The fact that our groups were not significantly different on listening skills points us in the direction of decoding for an explanation, sensible enough because decoding, as measured by nonword identification, was precisely the variable that distinguished the experimental and control groups.

A multiple regression analysis of the reading comprehension data confirms the plausibility of the Hoover and Gough (1990) model and of the suggestion that the experimental group's superiority lay in its advanced decoding skills. Listening comprehension accounted for 21% of the variance in reading comprehension, and nonword recognition added another highly significant 25% to that. Word identification processes that depend on knowing the spelling pattern of specific words, as reflected in the reading of irregular words such as *cough, plough*, and *knife*, added another 3% to bring the total variance accounted for to a substantial 49%, with over half attributable to processes operating at the single-word level.

The measure of print exposure, the Title Recognition Test (TRT), did not show any effect of either the experimental/control split or the passing/failing split. Nor did it relate to other variables in ways it might have been expected to. For instance, we could anticipate that the amount of print exposure that children had had would influence their recognition of irregularly spelled words, on the grounds that it is words like *lawn, sugar, flood,* and *knife* that most depend on reading experience because they do not decode readily. Yet the TRT score did not account for any of the variance in irregular reading performance after decoding (indexed by nonword reading) had been taken into account. (Irregular words are not completely arbitrary, and so knowledge of the relations between letters and sounds can be expected to influence their acquisition, something that fits the moderate correlations generally found between nonword reading and irregular word reading—see Freebody & Byrne, 1988; Byrne, et al., 1992.) Thus, it seems that the advantages the experimental group children were enjoying in reading progress had not translated into greater reading exposure, at least as far as the TRT was able to detect.

Evaluation: Grade 3.   The Grade 3 results, previously unpublished, tell a partly familiar and partly new story. A total of 105 children remained in the study, 57 from the experimental group and 48 from the control group. The comparison of the experimental and control groups showed again that decoding as tapped by nonword reading was superior in the experimental group; the respective means were 24.5 and 20.8/30, $t(103) = 2.56$, $P < .02$ (one-tailed test). None of the other tests, which included irregular word reading, reading comprehension, listening comprehension, and the TRT, produced a significant difference. The reclassification of the children into the preschool passing and failing groups again yielded a significant difference in word as well as nonword reading, with means out of 30 on word reading of 22.6 and 20.1 for the passing and failing groups, respectively, $t(103) = 1.82$, $P < .05$ (one-tailed test). This time, however, the measure of print exposure, the TRT, also revealed a pass/fail difference, with mean percentages of 35.2 and 26.5, $t(103) = 1.82$, $P < .05$ (one-tailed test).[3] The children who have all along been the better word readers now appear to be reading more. This is an example of Stanovich's (1986) "Matthew" effect in which early mastery of word recognition processes results in greater confidence with literature and therefore in greater exposure. We note, however, that the Grade 2 differential in reading comprehension did not reappear in Grade 3, suggesting that it may be a fragile phenomenon. Whether the newly emerged print exposure inequality will, in future years, magnify into further differentiation of the groups in basic reading processes, as Stanovich's "Matthew" effect would predict, remains to be seen.

Evaluation: Summary.   It is possible to teach phonemic awareness to preschool children using the vehicle of phoneme identity. The instruction, when combined with letter knowledge, helps them develop decoding skills, an advantage that remains with them throughout at least the first four years of school. Children who are phonemically aware on entering school also show advanced levels of word identification, and this translates into superior reading comprehension, for a while at least. There are signs that these children are also beginning to read more, something that may lead to further differentiation in the future.

The effects in the present study were not uniformly large, nor would we expect them to be. The schools in the study embraced a "mixed" reading curriculum, attending both to decoding skills through the use of "phonics" programmes and to reading for meaning in context. In so far as the schools were teaching the insights and aspects of knowledge that the preschool programme was aimed at, namely an appreciation of the segmental structure of speech and how the segments are represented by the letters of the alphabet, they were duplicating the aims of our experimental intervention. So the survival of any superiority for our experimental group is testimony to the early inculcation of phonemic awareness. Perhaps, too, it is evidence in favour of highly focused instruction in small groups, something that we will consider further in the next chapter.

OTHER RELEVANT INTERVENTION RESEARCH

There is now a sizeable collection of intervention studies with young children that incorporate some form of phonemic awareness training (e.g., Ball & Blachman, 1991; Bradley & Bryant, 1983; Cunningham, 1990; Hatcher, Hulme, & Ellis, 1994; Lundberg, Frost, & Petersen, 1988; O'Connor, Jenkins, & Slocum, 1995; Torgesen, Morgan, & Davis, 1992; Treiman & Baron, 1983; Vellutino & Scanlon, 1987). The studies vary considerably in subject characteristics, in what is taught and measured, and in the follow-up period. Despite this, it is commonly found that phonemic awareness can be taught and that such teaching leads to advances in decoding as assessed by nonword identification. It is also generally found that supplementing instruction in phonological structure with letter training enhances the difference between experimental and control groups. Thus, other research aligns with ours in indicating that acquisition of the alphabetic principle rests on the twin foundations of phoneme awareness and letter knowledge.

There is another way in which many of the other intervention research programmes and ours agree, and it is that gains in nonword reading are not always accompanied by gains in real word identification. Recall that our experimental group was not generally ahead of the controls on real words. Olson, Wise, Johnson, and Ring (1997) have summarised a variety of studies, including their own, and concluded that although gains in word identification sometimes accompany gains in nonword decoding (and phonological awareness), more often they do not. But other aspects of our results suggest that different ways of collecting and analysing data may paint a more encouraging picture about the consequences of early acquisition of the alphabetic principle. One aspect is the finding that the experimental/control split did produce a significant difference when infrequent words were tested separately (Grade 2). If this is a reliable finding, it suggests that superior decoders have the resources to become more independent readers by being able to decode words they may not have seen in print previously, i.e., infrequent words. Recall, too, that in our study word reading levels were often close to ceiling. In general, differences that are suppressed by tests with ceiling effects may be revealed by more difficult tests. Another consideration is that control groups may include children who have reached satisfactory levels of phonemic awareness without the benefit of the study's experimental intervention. Although the reclassification into phonemically aware and nonaware children mars the scientific purity of the research design, a case can be made for doing it. The case is simply that researchers do not usually insist that there is only one proper way to achieve phonemic awareness, namely via their particular teaching regimen, and so it makes sense to group together all the children who have done so. In the case of our project, this classification revealed long-lasting effects on word as well as nonword identification. The problem with this manoeuvre is that the re-assigned control children may have become good readers anyway, i.e., without the influence of phonemic awareness, and so one cannot be sure that phonemic awareness is the critical factor.

Most of the intervention studies reported so far have used more extensive and perhaps intensive instruction than the phoneme identity task we adopted. To take one example: O'Connor et al. (1995) used segmentation and blending for one group and those skills plus others such as rhyming and last-sound identity for another. Our choice of phoneme identity was justified earlier, and mainly hinged on the observations that identity was a more stable construct for preschoolers and that segmenting skill without accompanying insights into phoneme identity did not support good performance in the structured decoding test. We were also mindful of the tender age of our participants and of the necessity of not turning them off reading-like tasks. The children in the O'Connor et al. project were kindergarten age, presumably five years old. Looking for things beginning with /s/ seemed to us to be a gentler introduction to the world of phonology for four-year-olds than breaking words into phonemes or creating words from separately pronounced phonemes. Nevertheless, our data consistently told us that phoneme awareness (taught through phoneme identity) plus letter knowledge were necessary *but not sufficient* for decoding. Had we included the overt operations of segmenting and blending as well, we might have reduced the number of children who achieved the foundation skills but who still failed to decode, numbering 9 out of 45 at preschool (see Table 4.2). The message is that we still have much to learn about the best ways to teach phonemic awareness for children of different ages and with different levels of prior understanding.

CLASSROOM TEACHING PRACTICES

Other researchers have chosen to study literacy growth by capitalising on differences in classroom teaching strategies rather than (or as well as) instituting controlled intervention themselves. The most detailed work of this kind has been by Foorman and her group (e.g., Foorman & Francis, 1994; Foorman, Francis, Novy, & Liberman, 1991). They closely studied the reading and spelling progress of first-grade children in classes that varied in the amount of letter-sound instruction given. Foorman and her group found that more letter-sound instruction leads to faster growth rates in reading and spelling. In case studies of individual children, they also found that letter-sound instruction and phonemic segmentation ability act additively to promote reading and spelling (Foorman & Francis, 1994). By using the same words to test spelling across the year, the researchers found that the combination of progress in phonemic segmentation and more letter-sound instruction helped children move from errors that could be classed as *nonphonetic* to *phonetic* and then to correct spellings at a faster rate than children low in phonemic awareness and with less letter-sound instruction. The results are in line with those from controlled intervention studies.

REMEDIATION OF ESTABLISHED
READING DIFFICULTIES

Although the topic of severe reading retardation is well outside the scope of this book, it is nevertheless interesting that conclusions from controlled studies of remedial practices with children identified as reading-retarded converge with those from our intervention work. Research by Lovett and her colleagues (Lovett, Borden, DeLuca, Lacerenza, Benson, & Brackstone, 1994; Lovett, Borden, Warren-Chaplin, Lacerenza, DeLuca, & Giovinazzo,

1996; Lovett, Warren-Chaplin, Ransby, & Borden, 1990) provides a good example. As background, note that there is general agreement that much, though not all, of the difficulty dyslexic children face occurs at the level of the individual word, in particular in acquiring automatic word recognition skills, which underlie fluent reading (Lovett et al., 1996). Characteristically, these children can learn to identify a stock of words but appear not to extract the rules for pronouncing printed words that they have not practised. A child might learn *pine* and *shark*, for example, but may not be able to use the knowledge to help with unfamiliar words like *fine* and *bark* (Lovett et al., 1990—see also Byrne et al., 1997; Snowling, 1980). Deficiencies in phonemic awareness are thought to underlie this failure of generalisation. "... [G]iven a choice, the child with dyslexia will avoid subsyllabic segmentation and remain at a level of lexical analysis that does not challenge his or her areas of greatest deficit" (Lovett et al., 1994, p.818).

Lovett et al. (1994) report considerable success in teaching dyslexic children of around nine years of age to overcome this attested specificity in their word identification skills. The researchers were able to do this using a programme that emphasised the analysis of speech into its phonemic segments and the blending of those segments to form words, along with parallel instruction in the analysis and synthesis of print. (They also instituted another intervention that focused on word identification strategies such as locating parts of words to identify, removing affixes from the main word, and so on. These strategies improved word identification skills, although they were not as successful in helping with the decoding of nonwords as was the analysis/synthesis programme.) Lovett et al. (1994) concluded that "[t]he success of the present program must be attributed to the intensive training in phonological analysis and blending skills at the level of both oral and printed language .... Children with severe dyslexia can acquire and use letter-sound knowledge but ... this training success rests on embedding letter-sound training in an intensive phonological training program" (pp.818–819). The similarities of these claims to the message of this chapter, based on our intervention research, are clear.

LEARNABILITY THEORY

We began this chapter with a reminder that learning to read items in a writing system does not guarantee that learners will come to understand the organising principle of that system. So something needs to be added to Component 4 of Learnability Theory, information available to the learner. In this chapter we have traced a series of studies that have shown that in the case of alphabetic writing two things need to be included in Component 4. The first is information about the linguistic structures that the atomic elements of the system represent, phonemes. The second is specific information about which orthographic elements represent which linguistic elements, or letter-phoneme correspondences. From this base, most learners can decode new combinations of letters and begin the process of becoming skilled readers. The particular things that we taught the children were of a restricted nature, for example, phoneme identity for just a handful of phonemes. Yet we have evidence that the children generalised to other situations, for example, judging phoneme identity for untaught phonemes. This, plus the development of decoding skills for novel words and nonwords, tells us that learners make a great deal of progress on the basis of restricted information. Component 2, learning capacities, clearly includes processes that allow the child to go well beyond the data supplied by the environment. But from the data presented in the previous three chapters, what appears to be critical for triggering these powerful learning capacities is the correct initial hypothesis about the nature of the writing system. And if my interpretation is correct, that is not something that most children will arrive at unaided.

CHAPTER SUMMARY

In small-scale experiments reported in this chapter, preschool children showed the beginnings of decoding ability after they had achieved insight into the segmental structure of speech and had learned relevant letter-phoneme correspondences. Both phonemic awareness and letter knowledge were needed in combination for successful decoding. Other evidence indicated that teaching the concept of phoneme identity was the most effective way to instil phonemic awareness. Further data showed that phonemic awareness and the alphabetic principle are relatively robust once achieved: Most children could use them in situations other than the ones used for teaching them, although some preschoolers could not.

A programme to teach phoneme identity was developed and subjected to an evaluation trial. Children exposed to the programme in preschool ($N = 64$) were compared with a control group and showed superior decoding skills, as assessed by nonword reading, at the end of the instruction and throughout the succeeding four years of school. On occasions, the experimental group was ahead in word identification as well, and in Grade 2 in reading comprehension. When children were reclassified into those who left preschool with secure phonemic awareness and those who left without (three experimental group children were placed in the "fail" group and sixteen control group children were moved to the "pass" group), the former group showed advanced word identification skills throughout the entire evaluation. By Grade 3, the pass group appeared to be more experienced readers, as evidenced by their superior performance on a Title Recognition Test. All of these benefits were based on differences established in preschool, up to four years prior to the last reported testing.

Together, these data support the idea that children benefit from early, direct instruction in the segmental organisation of the speech stream. They also point to the importance of letter knowledge as the other foundation of the alphabetic principle. Our conclusions are reinforced by other groups' findings that instruction in phonemic awareness and letter knowledge benefits beginning readers and older children with established reading problems.

NOTES

1. Rack et al. (1994) choose to interpret their results in terms of children's sensitivity to the subphonemic feature matrix, something that may not reach conscious levels. They may well be correct, but other explanations are possible. For instance, English spelling itself might suggest to the children that using a z for the s in *basin* is reasonable enough because the evidence from words like *was* and *is* tells them that s and z may be interchangeable in spelling. But s and f do not interchange in this way. Other evidence that might support a climate of confusion over the "proper" way to spell and that might in particular muddy the waters when voicing rather than place of articulation is at stake are not hard to find; *of, lose, jumped* (the final sound is /t/, not /d/), *dogs* (voiced plural), *dirty* (in some dialects, the /t/ in *dirt* becomes closer to a /d/ in *dirty*). In addition, the phonetics of the voicing contrast may play a role. As well as the *dirt/dirty* example, where an unvoiced phoneme is phonetically voiced, "devoicing" of voiced phonemes can occur, particularly word-finally. So, for instance, the words *grief* and *grieve* are phonemically /grif/ and /griv/, but in casual speech the /v/ may be devoiced to become /f/. The difference between the two words is carried by vowel lengthening, which is correlated with word-final voicing. So phonetically the words become [grif] and gri:f]. If children are sensitive to these phenomena, as Read's (1971) work suggests, then they may not find using f to represent what we interpret as v, as in Rack et al.'s example *grfi* for *gravy*, difficult to accept.

2. These figures are slightly different from the ones appearing in Table 5 of Byrne and Fielding-Barnsley (1993a) because the phoneme identity scores in that original analysis were calculated on initial and final phonemes, not just the more discriminating final phonemes used here.

3. These are relatively conservative analyses, being based not on the individual child as the unit of analysis but on the means of the original preschool training groups, each of size 4 to 6. This procedure has strong justification (Levin, 1992), but it is worth noting that when the child is used as the unit of analysis the pass/fail comparisons are all significant under two-tailed tests. The analyses of previous grade results were also conducted using the teaching subgroup means as the units of analysis.

CHAPTER FIVE

Individual differences

Children vary in how easily they acquire the alphabetic principle. In this chapter, we search our data bases for clues as to the sources of this individual variation, and look, too, at other people's ideas and evidence. We also further trace the consequences for subsequent reading development of individual differences in grasp of the alphabetic principle. We will be particularly interested in low functional mastery of the principle as indicated by poor decoding skills, because that is believed to be the core problem for many older children with reading disabilities (Adams & Bruck, 1993; Share, 1995; Share & Stanovich, 1995; Stanovich, 1986).

We have already seen evidence of both these facets of individual differences, that is, differences in mastery of the alphabetic principle and variation in literacy development that spring from these initial differences. For example, in Chapter 2 we saw that a small proportion of children discovered that a discriminating letter in a word pair, like the *s* in the *hat/hats* contrast, represented a phoneme, whereas the majority remained blind to this function of the letter. In Chapters 3 and 4 we saw that some children had more difficulty than others in achieving insights into phonological structure, and that others acquired this building block of the alphabetic principle but failed to progress further, as evidenced by their failure to decode. We saw in the same chapter that having a firm grasp of the alphabetic principle, as indexed by good nonword reading, did not uniformly confer an advantage in terms of real word reading. Simultaneously, we saw that most children who understood the alphabetic principle by the end of preschool prospered in literacy development in the early school years. Thus, there are many questions about individual variation that invite answers. This chapter falls a long way short of providing all of these answers, though the data we have at hand do shed some light.

A FRAMEWORK FOR STUDYING INDIVIDUAL DIFFERENCES

We would not be surprised to discover that someone who had not attended school could not read, nor that someone born with profound mental deficiency could not read. These extreme cases exemplify what everyone intuitively recognises, that both experience and biological endowment can affect the acquisition of skills and abilities, reading included. In our search for causes of variation less dramatic than frank illiteracy, we should be alert for both environmental and constitutional factors. We must also acknowledge that the environment and biology interact in promoting or retarding literacy development. For instance, we will later see evidence for a sex difference in some of our variables, a superiority for girls. We may be tempted to ascribe the inequality to known differences between the male and female brain in regions specialised for language (Shaywitz et al., 1995), but other possibilities exist. For instance, parents might read more to girls than to boys. So the difference may be the result of environmental variation, which in turn is triggered by a biological difference.

In this chapter we will see that intensity of instruction, an environmental variable, exerts an influence on the development of phonological awareness. We will also see that genetics influences reading ability. Thus our intuition that experience and biological endowment both determine the course of literacy development is backed by hard evidence. Some authors consider that experiential factors should take centre stage in research, at least when considering reading disability. Spear-Swerling and Sternberg (1994, p.91) put things this way:

> Although both biological and environmental factors may interact in some cases of RD (reading disability), it is likely that more can be done to remedy a child's environment than his or her biology. Thus, in emphasising the importance of instructional, social and environmental factors in reading disability, we also emphasise the power that teachers have to improve the outlook of children with RD.

In my view, emphasising instruction is useful even if we acknowledge, as we must, that reading disability can be genetically determined. This is because we need to ascertain what kind and intensity of instruction is needed to ameliorate the effects of a deficient genetic endowment. I, too, have argued elsewhere that we should not be too ready to invoke biological and constitutional factors when the effects of environment may furnish satisfactory explanations for variation in aspects of literacy (Byrne, 1995). But how biology and experience interact will no doubt turn out to be a complex story, and from a scientific perspective all possibilities need to be considered.

In Learnability Theory terms, all components but Component 1, the target system, may be a source of individual variation. (In a comparison of different writing systems, the target system would need to be taken into account as well.) Different children might be endowed with different learning capabilities, or acquire them through experience (Component 2). They might be more or less willing to entertain particular hypotheses (Component 3). The learning environments may vary in influential ways (Component 4), and different children might be expected to reach different levels of mastery (Component 5). Thus the sources of individual variation are numerous.

OUR DATA BASES FOR STUDYING INDIVIDUAL DIFFERENCES

The data that our group have available include the studies summarised in the previous chapter plus two other investigations. Before turning to the main topic of this chapter, I will describe the rationale and methods of these two additional projects. The first one will also provide an opportunity to raise some issues about the assessment of phonemic awareness. The second was conceived as a direct investigation of one source of individual variation in young children, namely being a member of a family with a history of reading disability.

A new test of phoneme identity. The first study involved the development of a new test of phonemic awareness. The test was mentioned in Chapter 3, and the initial stages of the research are described in Byrne and Fielding-Barnsley (1993b). The test assessed phoneme identity, and used the familiar forced-choice format. A target item, such as *pig*, was presented with another item beginning with the same phoneme, *pool* in this example, and a foil, *beak*. As in our earlier test of phoneme identity, the items, which were all pictured, were identified for the children and they were asked to nominate the one that started the same as *pig*. The special feature of this test is that the foil (*beak*) is similar in sound, in a global way, to the target (*pig*), in fact as similar as the correct answer (*pool*) is to the target. The similarity is based on ratings of phoneme similarity made by adult judges, but you can get a feel for the outcome of the rating process by noting that *pig* and *beak* both begin with a bilabial stop, the vowels share articulatory gestures (both are high front vowels, terms which will be familiar to students of phonetics), and the final consonants, /g/ and /k/, share place of articulation and differ just in voicing, like the initial ones. The similarity between the target, *pig*, and the answer, *pool*, is founded on the identical initial phoneme. The reason for balancing global similarity was that it is known that children can base their judgements of phoneme identity on it. This can lead to the right answer for the wrong reasons in cases where the global similarity is confounded with phoneme identity (Treiman & Breaux, 1982), as illustrated later.

In our experimental analysis, we created a second set of items in which the foil was not much like the target. Instead of *beak* as the foil for *pig*, we used *shed*. Within the triplet *pig, shed, pool, pool* is more globally similar to the target *pig* by dint of its shared initial phoneme. This is an example of confounding shared phonemes and global similarity. We found that kindergarten children scored higher on the unbalanced version of the test, with *shed*-type items as the foils, than the balanced one, with *beak*-type foils. This tells us that "normal" tests of phoneme identity, which do not attend to the global similarity problem, may overestimate children's insights into identity at the segment level. Moreover, the balanced test (*beak*-type foils) correlated more highly with decoding and spelling performance of the kindergarten children, further testimony to its accuracy in assessing genuine understanding of phoneme identity. Cardoso-Martins (1994) has shown that children's judgements of rhyme can also be influenced by global similarity.

The new test just described comprised 20 balanced items for phoneme identity, and had an additional section, a recognition test for letter names. A letter name was read out and the children had to circle the correct letter in a row of four. Each of the 26 letters was tested this way. The children's performance on the phoneme identity part of the test was presented in graphic form in Fig. 3.3 in Chapter 3.

The data base relevant to the present chapter was created in a validation study of the new test. We administered it to 217 children in their second month in kindergarten, and six months later assessed the children who were still available for decoding and spelling skills. We used the same instruments as we had in the longitudinal project described in Chapter 4. One was a structured decoding in which a nonword, such as "ap", was read out and the child was required to indicate the correct printed form from three alternatives, *ap*, *ip*, and *aj*, in this example. The spelling test consisted of 10 common words, like *man* and *said*, and 4 nonwords, like *sut* and *yilt*. The results confirmed that phonemic awareness and alphabet knowledge both contribute to decoding and spelling in kindergarten (see Table 4.3 in Chapter 4 for earlier evidence). Together, phonemic awareness and alphabet knowledge accounted for 30% of the variance in decoding (alphabet, 28%; identity, a further and significant 2%) and 45% of the variance in spelling (40% plus 5%, respectively). (The total values are lower than the analogous figures from the evaluation study reported in Chapter 4, 40% and 56%, respectively. This is presumably because six months of teaching had intervened between the tests of phoneme identity and alphabet knowledge in the current case, whereas the testing was carried out simultaneously in the evaluation study.)

Early intervention for children at risk for reading disability. The second new data base is part of an ongoing study of children at risk for reading problems because of a family history of such difficulties. As pointed out earlier, there is now evidence implicating genetic factors in some cases of *dyslexia*, a cover term for reading and spelling disabilities. The evidence is partly behavioural, partly biological. The most comprehensive example of the former is a large-scale study of twins in Colorado (Olson, Forsberg, & Wise, 1994; Olson, Wise, Conners, Rack, & Fulker, 1989). At least one member of each twin pair recruited for the project was impaired in some way in reading ability. The question that the study addressed was whether identical twins are more similar in their reading and spelling patterns than are fraternal twins. Insofar as they are, there is evidence for an inherited component in the disability at the population level. The reasoning is based on the assumptions that identical twins share all their genes whereas fraternal twins share, on the average, half of their segregating genes, and that the two types of twins have equally similar environments. The Colorado research has concluded that there is indeed substantial genetic influence in dyslexia, with estimates of heritable variation in the range of 50–60% (DeFries & Gillis, 1991; Olson et al., 1994).

The direct biological data comes from mapping of Chromosome 6 in some of the participants in the Colorado studies (Cardon, Smith, Fulker, Kimberling, Pennington, & DeFries, 1994). A region on that chromosome linked to dyslexia was identified. Together, the two types of data make a strong case for genetic predisposition to reading problems.

It is not yet clear precisely how genetics may influence the processes that we have been concerned with in this monograph. We do know that phonological awareness, as measured by phoneme segmentation and transposition, has an h^2 (hereditability) value of around 60% in the Colorado sample (Olson et al., 1994). However, the youngest child was 8, and we cannot be sure that the same value, or indeed any significant value, would hold for younger children. It is also known that reading ability can influence performance on tests of phonemic awareness (e.g., Morais, Cary, Alegria, & Bertelson, 1979), so some of the similarity in phonemic awareness found among identical twins may be due to similarity in reading levels.

In addition, it is not known whether deficits in phonemic awareness are directly heritable, or come about because of deficits in some more basic mental process. To take an example: In an important and innovative paper, Fowler (1991) proposed that children vary in the "grain" of their underlying phonological representations. Some may store words as complete articulatory routines, incorporating consonants and vowels as integrated units at the level of the syllable. Others may store them as phonemic segments, which combine and recombine to form the large number of syllables and words in the vocabulary. Fowler's suggestion about the relation of underlying phonological representations and phonemic awareness is twofold; (a) that phonemic awareness will be limited by the degree of segmentation of the underlying lexical representations, and (b) that there is a developmental progression towards segmentation (accounting for age trends), with different children progressing at different rates (accounting for individual differences within ages). Conceivably, the rate of progression may be under direct genetic control. Alternatively, some other variable, itself subject to genetic influence, may be the critical factor. It has been proposed that children's representations of lexical items becomes increasingly segmented under pressure from vocabulary growth (Lindblom, 1986; Lindblom, MacNeilage, & Studdert-Kennedy, 1983; Walley, 1993), and it may be vocabulary acquisition that genes influence.

The purpose of this discussion is to illustrate that we have still a great deal to learn about genetic influences on the acquisition of the alphabetic principle. Nevertheless, it is not too early to begin investigating whether (and how) children who may be at risk for reading problems because of genetic factors can be helped through early intervention. This was the purpose of our project. At present, the best indicator that we have for the likelihood of a child being at risk for dyslexia is a family history of the disorder (other than in the rare case of a child who has a reading-disabled twin sibling). Even without the genetic data, it is known that children from affected families have an elevated risk of themselves developing reading problems (Gilger, Pennington, & DeFries, 1991; Scarborough, 1989). This by itself would justify early intervention. At the time of writing, the study is in its formative stages, but we do have data on 51 at-risk children who have participated in the first stage of the programme, and another 28 in the second stage (see later).

The children were selected for the study if they had a parent or older sibling with a marked reading problem and were to start school in the following year. Parental self-diagnosis was confirmed with standardised reading tests (only one family was eliminated because the "affected" parent in fact could read within normal limits), and older siblings were identified through school records. The intervention had three main facets, the phonemic awareness programme used in the longitudinal training study documented in Chapter 4, intensive training in the letters representing the phonemes used, and shared book reading. The book reading was modelled on a programme pioneered and researched by Whitehurst and his colleagues at Stony Brook (Whitehurst et al., 1988). It involves structured activities designed to engage the child in reading and to promote knowledge of print and of language skills. It is entitled *dialogic reading*.

The children were taught in groups of 2 to 6, depending for the most part on patterns of attendance at preschool. A few were taught individually. The number of weeks of instruction, at about 40 minutes per week in a single session, ranged from 16 to 20. We will examine aspects of the programme's outcome later, and further details are given in Byrne et al. (1997).

INDIVIDUAL DIFFERENCES IN ACQUIRING THE ALPHABETIC PRINCIPLE

Now we can return to the main theme, sources of individual differences in the acquisition of the alphabetic principle. We will first consider variation in how readily children acquire an understanding of the basic principles of alphabetic writing, and later trace some of the consequences of individual differences in this early stage for subsequent reading development. Our data provide information on a number of characteristics that have been linked to early progress in reading, and I will group them as follows: language-related variables of verbal IQ and productive vocabulary, and knowledge of rhyme; the biological variables of sex and family history of dyslexia; and a variable that perhaps belongs outside the traditional fold of individual differences but which demonstrably makes a differences to progress, namely intensity of instruction.

Verbal IQ.   We have been using the test of receptive vocabulary, the PPVT, as a proxy for verbal IQ, a strategy that is justified by the observation that vocabulary is the subtest with the highest correlation with overall verbal IQ (Sattler, 1988). In Chapter 4 we traced some of the relations between PPVT scores and the development of phoneme awareness. Briefly, the picture was that a relationship with phoneme identity was already established by the time we began working with the children in our intervention project, in the middle of their preschool year, but that the training effect (and more informal development in phoneme identity on the part of the control group children) was not further magnified by IQ differences. Nevertheless, the pretest data show that the level of children's verbal development, as measured by receptive vocabulary, correlates with their emerging awareness of the phonemic organisation of the speech stream.

In Chapter 4 we also saw that letter knowledge was part of the foundation for the acquisition of the alphabetic principle, along with phonemic awareness. The evidence for this was the dependence of decoding on both alphabet knowledge and phoneme identity. So to fill out the picture of the possible influence of verbal IQ on the alphabetic principle, we need to examine its correlations with letter knowledge. Pre-intervention, the PPVT correlated significantly with both letter name and letter sound knowledge, .38 and .41, respectively. It also correlated with knowledge of the six letters critical to the decoding task used post-intervention, a value of .32, and with the decoding measure itself, .23. However, the two foundations, letter knowledge and phonemic awareness, exhaust the influence of verbal IQ on decoding; together, letter knowledge and phonemic awareness account for 52% of the variance in decoding, but the PPVT adds nothing to the variance explained. So our data tell us that any effect of verbal IQ on emerging decoding is directed through the processes of letter knowledge and phonemic awareness.

We need to remember, of course, that all these data are correlational, and causal influence cannot be determined from them. It is plausible that some general factor is at work, underpinning vocabulary growth, knowledge of print, and metalinguistic awareness. In part, this overall process must be environmental, given that letter knowledge is tied up in it. But constitutional variation could also play a role, facilitating the influence of information provided by the child's social circumstances.

In contrast to the situation just described, data from the at-risk intervention project failed to show a relationship between receptive vocabulary and phonemic awareness. The correlation prior to any intervention was a nonsignificant .24, and with post-intervention phoneme identity it was just .17 (both $Ps > .05$, $N = 51$). Similarly, the

PPVT did not correlate significantly with any measure of alphabet knowledge in these children (r = .10, pre-intervention and r = .05, post-intervention). Not surprisingly, therefore, it did not correlate with a post-intervention measure of decoding (r = .08). However, some of these figures may not reflect population trends. In an extension of this study, a new group of 28 at-risk preschoolers has been tested, with pre-intervention data available at the time of writing. For this new group of children, the correlation between the PPVT and phoneme identity was .55 (P < .01). The correlation between the PPVT and alphabet knowledge was .35, which approached significance (P < .08). (It is worth pointing out that the PPVT-phoneme identity correlation of .24 for the main sample, reported earlier, also approached significance—it would have been significant on a one-tailed test.) We need further data with larger samples of at-risk preschoolers to be confident about the situation with these children, but there appears to be some reason to believe that for them, too, there is an early relationship between verbal IQ and phonemic awareness.

Returning now to the evaluation project described in Chapter 4: In kindergarten, one year after the preschool training programme, PPVT scores showed no influence on literacy. Even when entered first into regressions predicting word identification, decoding, and spelling, PPVT accounted for no significant portion of the variance (see Byrne & Fielding-Barnsley, 1993a, Table 5). Only once did the PPVT correlate significantly with word identification during three grades in which word identification was assessed, .30 with irregular word reading in Grade 3. It showed no reliable relationships with decoding of nonwords or the reading of regular words at any stage. In later years, however, the PPVT *did* show relationships with reading comprehension. The correlations between the PPVT and reading comprehension scores in Grades 2, 3, and 4 were .31, .46, and .46, respectively. Furthermore, the contribution of verbal intelligence to reading comprehension was in addition to the contribution of word-level identification processes. For instance, in Grade 3, decoding and identification of single words accounted for 31% of the variance in reading comprehension, and the preschool-administered PPVT added another 8%, for a total of 39%.

Thus, verbal intelligence, as tapped by preschool receptive vocabulary, does play a role in literacy development, at least in a "normal" sample of children. The PPVT correlates with early indications of phonemic awareness and letter knowledge, and so might be seen to affect indirectly the emergence of the alphabetic principle. But it seems that the educational process soon overwrites any influence of individual differences in general verbal ability as far as the further development of word identification processes is concerned. These differences do surface later as part of reading comprehension, however. It appears, therefore, that the primary influence of verbal ability is on higher-level processes (see also Stanovich, Cunningham, & Freeman, 1984). Its role in the acquisition of the alphabetic principle and the development of decoding is brief and limited.

Rhyme. In the previous chapter, I reported the study evaluating the preschool phonemic awareness program, *Sound Foundations*. We saw there that the pretest measure of rhyme correlated with post-intervention phonemic awareness, and that its influence extended beyond that of pretest phonemic awareness. For the children as a whole, it added an extra 7% to the 17% of variance explained by pretest phoneme identity alone (and 3% to the 66% of variance explained by group membership plus pretest phoneme identity). In the experimental group, the relative figures were 23% and 8% (pretest phoneme identity and rhyme), and for the control group they were 51% and 4% (see Chapter 4 for a comment on the disparity between the absolute size of these figures for the two groups). Thus, children's sensitivity to rhyme partially underpins further growth in phonological awareness at the level of the segment, whether that growth is the result of intensive instruction or not.

For most children, rhyme sensitivity develops prior to segment sensitivity (Goswami & Bryant, 1990, 1992; Liberman et al., 1974), and continues to predict reading scores for several years (Bradley & Bryant, 1985; Bryant et al., 1989). The data reported in Chapter 4 suggest that part of the effectiveness of rhyme is attributable to its influence on phonemic awareness. This conclusion is supported by the fact that rhyme did not account for any more variance in the preschool decoding scores over and above the 38% accounted for by post-intervention phoneme identity, even though it correlated significantly with decoding $(r = .34)$.

However, preschool rhyming ability does not just influence later reading and spelling performance via its effect on phonemic awareness. In kindergarten, adding rhyme as a predictor of spelling after post-intervention phonemic awareness has been entered raises the variance accounted for from 15% to 24%. Rhyme even accounts for significant variance when added after phoneme identity assessed at the same time as spelling (i.e., in kindergarten). Here the analogous values are 28% and (an extra) 5%. Rhyme did not, however, contribute significantly to the explanation of variance in word recognition and decoding in kindergarten on top of phoneme identity. But rhyme's influence continues to emerge in later years in our longitudinal sample. In Grade 1, it increased variance explained in spelling from the 15%

attributable to phoneme identity (measured in Grade 1) by a further 9%. As in kindergarten, word identification and nonword decoding were not influenced independently by rhyme, but in Grades 2 and 3 rhyme did explain independent variance in the identification of *irregularly* spelled words. In both grades, the additional variance accounted for was 5%. In neither grade did rhyme account for independent variance in nonword reading, nor, in Grade 2, in regularly spelled word identification (this was not tested in Grade 3). Recall that rhyme was tested early in preschool, so its continuing influence up to four years later is testimony to its importance.

All of these data are, of course, correlational, and therefore their interpretation is bedevilled by the usual complications. However, they are broadly in line with the view that rhyme sensitivity provides the phonological grounding for the development of advanced orthographic knowledge (Goswami & Bryant, 1990). This is thought of as being based on letter groups representing phoneme groups, often centred on rhyme. So, the word *night* loses some of its apparent irregularity when its similarity to *right, fight*, and *light* is noted. This similarity will only register on children who recognise the shared rime portion of the spoken words. Early availability of rhyming capacity will presumably give the child an advantage in building up orthographic knowledge and therefore a stock of rapidly recognised "sight" words. In this context, it is interesting that our data show an effect of rhyme on irregular words but not on regular ones or on nonwords. If *irregularity* is defined at the level of individual letters, *night* can be categorised as irregular, but this categorisation loses some of its force at the letter-group level, as *night* and its orthographic neighbours show. Others have also suggested that rhyme becomes more important in more advanced stages of literacy development, a conclusion that is consistent with our data (Bowey & Hansen, 1994; Coltheart & Leahy, 1992; Treiman, Goswami, & Bruck, 1990; Wimmer, Landerl, & Schneider, 1994).

To summarise, it appears that the ability to notice rhyme relations among words plays a double role in explaining individual differences in the course of literacy development. In the early stages, rhyme promotes an appreciation of the smaller phonological unit, the phoneme, perhaps by providing a focus on the form as opposed to the meaning of words. Detecting relations at the more accessible rhyme level may provide a stepping stone to detecting relations at the segment level (Bryant et al., 1989). At later stages, an appreciation of rhyme may underpin the development of orthographic knowledge, particularly for those many sequences in English that are irregular at the phoneme-grapheme level, but which exhibit more consistency at the rhyme level, such as *ight, tion*, and *ought*.

Sex. It has long been observed that boys are over-represented in reading disability classes and clinical samples. There is some doubt whether this sex imbalance represents a genuine ability difference in boys and girls or is more the product of referral processes in which boys with reading problems are more noticeable in class than girls with similar difficulties, and are therefore more readily singled out for special treatment (see Shaywitz, Shaywitz, Fletcher, & Escobar, 1990, for some evidence to this effect). With the relatively large numbers of children in our data bases, we are in a position to inquire whether sex is a contributor to variation in the acquisition of the alphabetic principle, before referral for help becomes an issue. If it is, then the imbalance may well be based on a real difference in reading skill rather than referral practices.

The preschool means for boys and girls who participated in the training study reported in Chapter 4 are shown in Table 5.1, along with tests of significance. There was a highly significant difference in favour of girls in the Concepts About Print (CAP) test and, among the post-intervention measures, a borderline female superiority in decoding and knowledge of the six critical letters. The first of these results suggests that girls are exposed more to the world of books, or absorb more information from the same exposure as boys. This may spill over into a more secure knowledge of letters, although better letter knowledge was not characteristic of girls in the pretests. The absolute difference in favour of girls on letter sounds is significant on a one-tailed test at $P < .05$, but firmer evidence for a sex difference in letter knowledge comes from the data base generated during the trials of the balanced test of phoneme identity. Recall that this involved testing 217 children, 96 of whom were girls and 121 were boys, in the first month of kindergarten. Girls knew an average of 16.5 letters, boys an average of 13.4, $t(215) = 3.50$, $P < .001$. (We did not collect CAP data on these children.) So there appears to be a case for claiming that in culturally determined aspects of early literacy, namely knowledge of the conventions of printed language and of letters, girls are ahead of boys. They were in these samples, anyway.

This conclusion must be tempered by the observation that boys knew more environmental signs, such as *Stop* and *McDonalds*, than girls did (see Table 5.1). It is not clear how to reconcile these two findings, except to say that because both must depend to a degree on responsiveness to exposure to various literacy sources we might search for differences in broader life habits for an explanation.

Table 5.1 shows that girls performed better than boys on the preschool structured test of decoding (does *sat* say "sat" or "mat?", etc). This is probably due to their more secure knowledge of the critical letters. In a

TABLE 5.1
Means of preschool girls and boys: pre-intervention measures

Group	Phoneme identity	Rhyme	Letter names	Letter sounds	Concepts about print	Common signs
Girls	24.5	7.2	13.4	6.6	6.2	2.4
Boys	23.2	7.1	12.2	4.6	4.8	2.8
t-test	0.35, n.s.	0.76, n.s.	0.44, n.s.	1.71, $P < .05$ (one-tailed)	2.64 $P < .01$	2.07 $P < .05$

Means of preschool girls and boys: post-intervention measures

Group	Phoneme identity	Critical letters	Decoding
Girls	35.6	4.0	7.7
Boys	33.9	3.3	6.8
t-test	0.37, n.s.	1.93, $P < .05$ (one-tailed)	1.98, $P < .05$

regression analysis, sex added nothing to the 43% variance in decoding that letter knowledge accounted for. We see something similar at work in the kindergarten data collected on the children to whom we gave the new phoneme identity and alphabet test. We gave decoding and spelling tests to the 182 we could readily locate six months after the original testing, and found that girls were better spellers than boys (means of 52.8 and 45.9, respectively, $t(180) = 2.08, P < .05$; there was no significant difference on the decoding test). However, the sex variable did not add at all to the 40% of variance in spelling accounted for by alphabet knowledge, indicating that its effect was mediated by alphabet familiarity.

No data suggested a sex difference in phonemic awareness. Table 5.1 shows no differences between boys and girls in either the pretest or posttest of phoneme identity. Likewise, in the kindergarten validation of the new phoneme identity test, the difference between boys and girls did not approach significance (means of 12.6 and 13.1, respectively, $t(215) = 0.98, P > .20$). Thus, our data suggest that any sex differences that might emerge as children develop in literacy do not have their origins in differential appreciation of the phonemic structure of speech. Instead, they start as a result of a female superiority in letter knowledge and in print conventions.

However, the sex difference in the evaluation study described in Chapter 4 was short-lived; sex did not generate significant performance differences in any of the later measures of literacy, at the individual word level, in comprehension, or in print exposure. All probability levels in tests of significance from kindergarten to Grade 3 were beyond .20. In addition, no sex differences emerged when numbers of children falling below −1 standard deviations on the various measures of word identification and on comprehension were tabulated. Boys were not over-represented at the low end of the distributions. The point of this analysis is that equal average performance can hide differences at the extremes. Because we are often interested in children whose performance puts them at the bottom of their grade, and because boys outnumber girls in remedial classes, we need to give our data the chance to reveal a sex imbalance in the lowest-performing groups that may be submerged in a comparison of means and may underlie the referral differential. But no imbalance emerged.

The failure to find a sex effect beyond the preschool level does not mean that differences might not be found in other samples, especially ones in which half of the children have not had the advantage of intensive preschool phonemic awareness training. Indeed, as already noted, girls performed at a higher level than boys on spelling in kindergarten in the validation study, probably reflecting a superiority in alphabet knowledge detected six months earlier. So in total our data support the possibility but not the certainty of a female advantage in literacy development. When a female advantage does occur, however, it does not appear to be based on differences in phonemic awareness but rather on differences in familiarity with printed language, including letters.

Family history of dyslexia. The at-risk study, introduced earlier, examines one potential marker of individual differences in early reading development, namely the presence or absence of a family history of marked reading difficulties. We can draw only limited and tentative conclusions from our data so far because we do not have a dedicated control group of children to match the at-risk children on important variables like socio-economic level (see Bowey, 1995). Furthermore, some of the tests we have used with the at-risk children differ from those administered to others with whom some comparison is possible, such as the children in the evaluation study described in Chapter 4. For instance, we used our "balanced" test of phoneme identity (see earlier) with the at-risk children instead of the original test used in the evaluation study because of its superior conceptual basis. Nevertheless, we can make some comparisons with the longitudinal evaluation trial, as well as checking for correlates of development just within the at-risk group (see the earlier discussion of productive vocabulary). The chapter by Byrne et al. (1997) describes some of these comparisons, summarised next.

TABLE 5.2
Pre-instruction performance of at-risk and "normal" preschoolers

Variable (and statistic)	At-risk children	"Normal" children
Rhyme[a] (mean)	5.4	7.2
CAP[b] (mean	3.8	5.4
Phoneme identity (% children passing)	8	29

[a] Maximum = 10. [b] Concepts about print.

The at-risk children showed deficiencies in three fundamental variables measured prior to instruction. The data are in Table 5.2. The tests which are identical in form across both groups of children are Rhyme and Concepts About Print, and on both the at-risk children had lower means than the children from the original evaluation trial (whom I will now refer to with the shorthand title of "normal"). The phoneme identity data are expressed in terms of percentages because of the use of different test formats. A smaller proportion of at-risk children exhibited competence in this skill. So already we have evidence that children who have a parent or older sibling with a marked reading problem are behind at age four on some variables known to be related to early literacy development.

The at-risk children responded to the instruction, not surprising given its intensity but encouraging nevertheless. In Table 5.3 are the pre- and post-instruction means for four variables, and all showed increases with probabilities beyond .001. It is also encouraging that the at-risk children performed as well as the normal children on the post-instruction measure of emerging decoding skill (does *sat* say "sat" or "mat?"). Their mean was 8.0 (chance = 6, maximum = 12; the normals' score was 8.2, not significantly higher). This good performance was

TABLE 5.3
Pre- and post-instruction mean scores for at-risk preschoolers on four variables

Variable	Pre-instruction	Post-instruction
Phoneme identity (max = 20, chance = 10)	10.9	14.6
Rhyme awareness (max = 10, chance = 3.3)	5.4	7.3
Letter names	9.2	13.5
Concepts about Print	3.8	8.1

attained despite lower levels of achievement in phoneme identity (see later), and seems to have been influenced by very secure knowledge of the six letters critical to the task (mean score of 5.1 against the normals' 3.9). This difference reflects the extra attention devoted to letter knowledge in the at-risk group's instructional regimen, and tells us that learning the sounds of letters does not appear to pose special difficulties for at-risk children as a group, at least when the instruction is intensive. Even with our highly focused teaching, however, 13/51 (25%) of the at-risk children were less than secure on these six letters, with scores of four or less (11 of these scored three or less). We do not have a standard against which to judge this figure of 25% because letter knowledge for the main training study's group was taught incidentally rather than directly. But it remains possible that learning the names and/or sounds of letters represents a trouble spot for some at-risk children. Future research should address this important question.

Although the training regimens for the at-risk and normal children were not the same in all respects—the at-risk group received more intensive letter training and engaged in dialogic reading— the relative contributions to decoding from letter knowledge and phonemic awareness were very similar across the two groups. The relevant figures are given in Table 5.4. It appears that at-risk children utilise their basic understanding of phonological structure and knowledge of letter-sound correspondences to underpin print decoding in the same kind of way as normal children do. Just like the normals, they rely on the combination of phonemic awareness and alphabet to support decoding. This is also encouraging news; once basic knowledge is available to at-risk children, their progress in the early stages of reading acquisition proceeds as normal. This in turn suggests that the first place to focus in intervention is on these foundation insights and knowledge, phonemic awareness and letter-sound correspondences. Of course, the possibility of continuing

TABLE 5.4
Prediction of post-instruction decoding from letter knowledge and phonemic awareness in at-risk and "normal" preschoolers

	Variable	R^2 change	
		At-risk children (n = 51)	Normal children (n = 125)
Step 1	Letter knowledge	.40	.43
Step 2	Phonemic awareness (phoneme identity)	.16	.11
Total		.56	.54

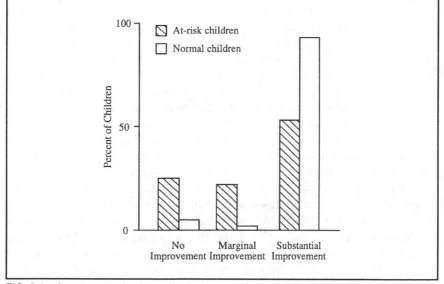

FIG. 5.1.   Improvement in phonemic awareness after preschool intervention for at-risk and normal children.

difficulties that are due to processes entering reading mastery at later stages is not ruled out by this analysis. Still, as far as a functional knowledge of the alphabetic principle is concerned, at-risk children seem to progress in the same way as other children.

Here, however, is the bad news about this sample of at-risk children. As shown in Fig. 5.1, they were less responsive to instruction in phoneme identity than were the normal children. Even though for the at-risk children the intervention was more extensive, including as it did the shared book reading and letter training, 25% showed no growth in phonemic awareness across the period of instruction compared with just 5% of the normal sample. The respective figures for substantial improvement (to well above chance values) were 53% (at-risk group) and 93% (normals). Of the at-risk children, 22% could be classed as showing only partial improvement, compared with just 2% of the normals. In summary, a quarter of the at-risk children did not benefit from instruction that helped nearly all of an unselected sample of preschoolers, and another one-fifth showed only marginal improvement compared to just one in fifty of the normal sample.

These last data suggest that a sample of children from families with a history of reading problems will contain a higher than normal number who are relatively unresponsive to instruction in one of the foundations of the alphabetic principle, the phonemic organisation of the speech stream. It is interesting to note that the two extreme groups, the children showing no improvement (NI) and those showing substantial improvement (SI), did not differ on the *pre*-instruction measure of phoneme identity; means of 11.0 and 11.2, respectively. It seems that the post-instruction difference may reflect a dynamic variable, teachability, and not a static one indexed by pre-existing levels of phonemic awareness. The teachability referred to may be specific to phonemic awareness; on three other variables measured before and after instruction, rhyme awareness, letter name knowledge for all 26 letters, and Concepts About Print, both groups—NI and SI—improved to about the same extent. However, the SI group did outperform the NI group on the six critical letters (means of 5.7 and 4.5, respectively, $F(1, 38) = 7.91$, $P < .01$), so it is not just phoneme identity change that differentiates these two groups. Our test for letter knowledge on this occasion was the ability to give the sounds rather than the names of the six letters (in conformity with our earlier longitudinal evaluation study), and therefore the children's poorer performance may have been a direct consequence of not having acquired a grasp of these phonemes as objects.

These data are only suggestive, but future research with at-risk children could profitably include measures of teachability and not just measures that give a single time-slice of skill and metalinguistic levels. It is, after all, a failure to learn that is the mark of reading disability, and learning is a dynamic process.

In summary, at-risk children already show deficiencies at age four on variables known to be related to progress in literacy development, namely phonological awareness, letter knowledge, and familiarity with the conventions of printed language. The children can be taught these important skills and ideas, though they appear to be less responsive in some ways than normal children. In particular, phonemic awareness did not advance in a substantial minority of our sample, and a hypothesis worth exploring is that the source of the differences between at-risk and normal children lies in teachability of the core concept of phonemic organisation. In this minority of at-risk children, knowledge of the letters that represent the phonemes they failed to learn about was also compromised, perhaps because the phonemes that the letters correspond to were not accessible objects for them. However, once the foundations for discovery of the alphabetic principle *are* in place, at-risk children appear to advance to decoding in the same way as normal children. Their problems may primarily be centred on achieving the foundations in the first place.

Instructional arrangements.   A central point of the previous chapters is that children do not necessarily discover the alphabetic principle for themselves, even when they learn to read words arranged to reveal this principle. Children mostly need to be taught about how alphabets represent spoken language. Therefore, it is reasonable that among the factors contributing to individual differences in alphabetic mastery will be how children are taught, in particular the intensity of the instruction. We do not have a systematic study of this factor, but our data do have something to say about it.

We were interested to check on the effectiveness of the phonemic awareness training programme we developed, *Sound Foundations*, when delivered in regular classrooms by preschool staff working from the programme's manual (see Byrne & Fielding-Barnsley, 1995, for a full report of this study). Recall that in our evaluation trials the children had been taught in groups of 4 to 6, all by one instructor (Ruth Fielding-Barnsley). The utility of the programme for normal use is not guaranteed by the promising results of those trials because the instruction was at a level of intensity unlikely to be recreated in normal preschool environments. So we invited three preschools to implement the programme in whatever ways best fitted the schools' schedules. We wanted to examine its performance under normal classroom use. We explained the aims of the programme, and urged the staff to keep those aims in mind when working with the children. Other than that, we did nothing except provide copies of the manual and the teaching materials.

When we interrogated the preschool staff at the end of this new trial, we found that implementation contrasted with the original evaluation study in several ways. One was in the size of the teaching groups. In the preschools, they were mostly around 20. A second contrast was in how the teaching materials were used. There was consistent use of the posters, but some teachers did not introduce the card games, and others made only sparse use of them. Third, all three preschools taught initial sounds but only one taught final sounds. Thus, the intensity of instruction delivered to any single child probably fell below the level available to the experimental group in the main evaluation study; the children were in larger groups and they had fewer learning opportunities.

We first needed to compare the children's performance with the original control group to check whether the classroom-based delivery worked at all. It did. There was more pre- than post-instruction improvement in phoneme identity in the classroom group than in the control group, but only for initial sounds (see Fig. 5.2). When we examined individual children, we discovered that the number who passed the test of phoneme identity (defined as 32 correct out of a maximum of 48 in the test, 67%) went from 20% prior to instruction to 51% after instruction in the classroom group compared with a shift from

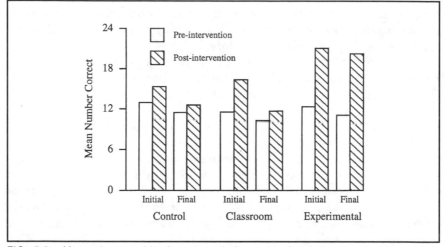

FIG. 5.2.   Mean phoneme identity scores before and after instruction for the control, classroom, and experimental groups.

22% to just 31% in the control group, a significant difference favouring the classroom group.

The failure to find added improvement for final sounds for the classroom groups makes sense because only one of the preschools taught were final sounds. (In the one that did, performance went from a mean of 10.9 to 16.7 out of 24, whereas in the two that did not, the maximum increase was just 1.0.) But this aspect of the data tells us that an understanding of phoneme identity does not necessarily generalise from initial sounds to final ones if it is taught using initial sounds. In Chapter 4 we saw that phoneme identity *did* generalise from the sounds that were used as examples in instruction to *other sounds*, but it appears that position is more training-dependent. We also saw in Chapter 4 that once children knew the letters corresponding to phonemes and could decode these letters in new words, decoding performance was largely independent of position in which the insights were trained. The present failure of generalisation, then, suggests that phoneme identity, as a "bare" insight unsupported by letter knowledge, can be fragile; it is position-dependent (though not phoneme-dependent). Once the idea of phoneme identity is supplemented by letter knowledge, it gains in robustness; it is no longer position-dependent. This constitutes yet another reason to package the teaching of phonemic awareness and letter knowledge together; doing so stabilises phonemic awareness.

Returning to the main theme: The comparison with the original experimental group provides the test of the idea that intensity of instruction is important in the development of phonemic awareness in young children. From Fig. 5.1 it can be seen that the mean levels of improvement in the original experimental group outstripped those of the classroom group, an observation confirmed by statistical analysis (see Byrne & Fielding-Barnsley, 1995). The percentage of children in the experimental group passing the test of phoneme identity rose from 20% to 95%, pre- to post-instruction (compared with 20% and 51% in the classroom group). Thus, the classroom instruction of the new trial resulted in fewer children achieving high levels of phonemic awareness. This is consistent with the hypothesis that intensity of training is one factor in the child's awareness of phonemic organisation, one of the foundations of the alphabetic principle.

Of course, there are other differences between the experimental group of the original evaluation trial and the classroom group of the new trial. Perhaps most prominent is the teacher difference. It is possible that the classroom preschool teachers would have generated the same (more modest) levels of improvement even if they had taught the children under precisely the same conditions as had Ruth Fielding-Barnsley. That is, there may be a pure teacher effect. Our data do not allow us to adjudicate this possibility.

Moreover, even if the term *intensity of instruction* correctly characterises the crucial variable, it is probably not accurate to think of this as a continuous variable, analogous to an athlete's training schedule where there is a reliable relationship between time at the training track and ultimate performance. Grasping the idea of phoneme identity tends to be an all-or-none affair, as evidenced by the fact, documented in Chapter 4, that once it is achieved for some phonemes it spreads unaided to others (but see the earlier discussion about position generalisation). In working with children, we notice that some children seem to understand phoneme identity quite quickly once the fact that different words can start with the same sound is brought to their attention; others fail to see phoneme identity for a long time when it is staring them in the face in instructional sessions. Thus, intensity of training is more akin to being able to monitor individual children closely, tailoring the teaching to their current levels of understanding, motivational states, attentional resources, and so on. This level of attention is precisely what is hardest to achieve when children are being taught in large groups and with a restricted range of material resources.

Summary and review. This completes our survey of sources of individual differences contributing to the child's acquisition of the alphabetic principle. In fact, we have extended the survey to include aspects of literacy progress after the basics have been mastered (or not mastered), as in the observations about the influences of IQ, sex, and rhyme awareness on later literacy development. The latter discussion is extended below. We have seen that differences in vocabulary, as measured by the PPVT, go hand in hand with differences in phonemic awareness and in letter knowledge, thereby underpinning emerging decoding skills. Another linguistic variable, awareness of rhyme, also correlates with early phonemic awareness and therefore also contributes indirectly to preschool decoding ability. The one truly biological variable we examined, sex, may play a role in the discovery of the alphabetic principle, but via a social route. Girls showed signs of greater familiarity with printed language, including letter names, though they did not have higher levels of phonemic awareness than boys and were not more responsive to instruction than boys. Another variable over which children have no control, family history of reading difficulties, was seen to influence early literacy development. Preschoolers with a parent or older sibling with a marked reading problem tended to score lower on phonological awareness, letter knowledge, and familiarity with print, and tended to be less responsive to instruction in phonemic awareness. And finally, instruction itself is important. The more intensive it is, the more children prosper in phonemic awareness.

These sources of variation, and others not covered in this chapter, doubtless influence early literacy development in different ways. Sex, for example, leaves phonemic awareness untouched, according to our data, yet affects early signs of decoding through its influence on letter knowledge. Rhyme awareness probably assists early decoding through its effect on phonemic awareness and not through a direct effect on letter knowledge. It is also likely that those variables that affect one of the foundations of the alphabetic principle, phonemic awareness, say, do so in different ways. If vocabulary size plays a causal role, it may be because of the "phonemicisation" that an enlarged lexicon imposes on the internal representation of words, as suggested by Fowler (1991). On the other hand, intensity of instruction obviously works in a different and direct way on phonemic awareness. Rhyme awareness may exert its influence by sensitising children to words as phonological sequences, paving the way for the discovery of smaller, phonemic units.

As yet, we have no unified theory integrating the sources of individual differences. However, Learnability Theory provides at least a framework for classifying the sources. For a start, we can divide the sources of individual differences into those that ultimately are extrinsic to the child and those that are intrinsic. It is Component 4, the learning environment, that accommodates extrinsic variation. This might include intensity of instruction, which we considered earlier, and other things like word play (rhyming and alliteration games, for instance; Dowker & Pinto, 1993) and book reading (Whitehurst et al., 1988), which may be part of family life. Intrinsic factors would belong in Component 2, the learning capabilities of the child, and Component 3, hypotheses entertained. Learning capabilities might exhibit individual variation along lines we have already considered. For instance, in Chapter 4 we saw that most children could decode a letter in a word-final position whose phonological value they had learned in word-initial position, but some could not. We also saw that most children understood the idea of phoneme identity for phonemes that had not been part of the instruction, but presumably some children did not make the appropriate generalisation. Thus, there may be a variable, which we could call *specificity of learning*, that influences discovery of the alphabetic principle and early literacy progress. Some children may generalise readily, others less readily. As another example of likely intrinsic variation, recall the evidence from Chapter 3 that a minority of preschoolers noticed the phonological value of letters like the *er* in *smaller* whereas the majority did not. We do not yet know the source of this variation in Component 3 of Learnability Theory, hypothesis formation, but it is likely to prove important in tracing different paths children follow in discovering the basic phonological nature of English writing. The ability to focus on the form as distinct from the meaning of words may be part of a more general ability to *decentre*, a Piagetian concept adapted for the case of literacy acquisition by Tunmer (see Tunmer & Hoover, 1992, for an overview).

These examples of individual variation could be multiplied many times over, and as I have pointed out elsewhere (Byrne, 1992) most characteristics that differentiate one child from another have at some time been linked to variation in literacy acquisition. I believe that we can only bring order to this collection of hypotheses in the context of some well-worked-out model of the acquisition process. In this volume I have tried to present an account of an early stage of literacy mastery, the discovery of the alphabetic principle. The main burden of the argument has been that this discovery rests on the twin foundations of an understanding of the phonemic organisation of the speech stream and knowledge of how (and which) letters represent the phonemes. It follows, according to this account, that individual differences that affect the discovery of the alphabetic principle must flow through one or both of these foundations. They form the final common path, to borrow a term from pharmacology, to the alphabetic principle. Empirical and conceptual analyses of individual differences can be constrained by models such as this one.

EFFECTS OF EARLY VARIATION IN MASTERY OF
THE ALPHABETIC PRINCIPLE ON LATER
READING DEVELOPMENT

In this final section, I take variation in mastery of the alphabetic principle as input and examine subsequent progress in literacy. We have already seen some of that story in Chapter 4, where it was clear that children given explicit instruction in phonemic organisation in preschool became better decoders in kindergarten and exhibited further signs of good reading over the next three years. Our data have their counterparts in other intervention studies, reviewed briefly in previous chapters. There also exist excellent reviews of how getting off to a good start in reading (i.e., early mastery of the alphabetic principle) leads to later reading competence (e.g., Share, 1995; Share & Stanovich, 1995; Stanovich, 1986), and considerable evidence that children remain in approximately the same rank order in reading ability across their school careers (Juel, 1988; Shaywitz et al., 1995). There is also evidence that phonological awareness deficits persist as accompaniments to poor reading into adulthood (Bruck, 1990).

The data from our group confirm that there is stability in rank order of children's reading levels across school grades, but suggest some modifications to that picture that add to the hypothesis that decoding skills play an especially significant role in reading progress. The data come from longitudinal and cross-sectional analyses of reading scores, reported in Freebody and Byrne (1988) and in Byrne et al. (1992). The research was undertaken in the context of claims that some readers could be classified as inordinately dependent on a "sight" vocabulary, without accompanying high levels of decoding skills, whereas others had low stocks of sight words and instead relied on a more laborious letter-by-letter decoding strategy (Baron, 1977, 1979; Baron & Strawson, 1976; Baron & Treiman, 1980). The theoretical context that allows for strategy differences in readers is provided by so-called *dual route* models of skilled reading, which hold that words can be identified either by grapheme-phoneme correspondence rules or as wholes (Coltheart, Davelaar, Jonasson, & Besner, 1977). Some of the motivation for dual-route theory derives from the fact that there are many English words, like *laugh*, *aisle*, and *pint*, that cannot be read accurately by pronouncing individual letters—hence the need for word-level identification processes. But people can also read print sequences that they have never seen before, like *flub*, *lemat*, and *pilk*, so word-level memorisation processes will not do a complete job. This class of model is also supported by the literature on acquired dyslexia, in which there are reports of selective impairment to one of the routes along with sparing of the other in cases of adults whose reading and spelling skills have been affected by brain injury or disease. There are people who can read *laugh* but not *lemat*, and people who can read *lemat* but not *laugh* (see Coltheart, Curtis, Atkins, & Haller, 1993, for a review of these kinds of cases and a defence of dual-route theory). Evidence for counterparts of these differing forms of dyslexia in children has been provided by some researchers (e.g., Castles & Coltheart, 1993), although there are disagreements of interpretation on this issue (Bryant & Impey, 1986; Snowling, Bryant, & Hulme, 1996; Stanovich, Siegel, & Gottardo, 1997). There also exist sophisticated single-route models of skilled reading based on parallel distributed computing techniques (Seidenberg & McClelland, 1989; Plaut, McClelland, Seidenberg & Patterson, 1996), which compete with dual-route theory. This debate, focused as it is primarily on skilled reading, is mostly beyond the scope of this monograph. But its early stages, and the possibility that different degrees of dependence on one route or the other occur, provided part of the rationale for the studies by Freebody and Byrne (1988) and Byrne et al. (1992).

Parenthetically, it might be argued that if there are two independent routes to identifying written words, direct access on the basis of the whole word and indirect access on the basis of grapheme-phoneme correspondence rules, and if readers are free to, and do, choose the direct route (as the idea of strategy implies), then the entire rationale for this book disappears. Direct access does not involve use of, and therefore does not require an understanding of, the alphabetic principle. However, no adherent of dual-route theory, to my knowledge, has suggested that there is exclusive use of one route even in skilled reading, and none has suggested that exclusive use of the direct route occurs during reading acquisition. Correspondence rules, and therefore the alphabetic principle on which they rest, need to be incorporated in the repertoire of reading skills. In any case, there is good evidence that the two routes are not independent: There are substantial correlations between the ability to read exception words like *laugh* and *aisle*, likely to be the province of direct access, and the ability to read nonwords like *flub* and *lemat*, which can only be read by correspondence rules (Freebody & Byrne, 1988; Treiman, 1984); children who are better decoders are better able to learn new exception words (Gough & Walsh, 1991); and even at the very beginnings of their apprenticeships as readers, children unavoidably exploit grapheme-phoneme correspondences in learning new words (Ehri, 1992). Gough, Juel, and Griffith (1992, p.44) summarise much of this evidence by noting that it "suggests that word-specific knowledge, rather than being deployed in a separate mechanism, is instead gathered within the same mechanism with the cipher. Metaphorically, it is assembled 'on top of' the cipher". Ehri (1992) has produced the most detailed model to date of how children acquire a reading vocabulary within a single framework, one that critically depends on the discovery of the alphabetic principle. Thus there are good reasons for believing that, whatever the case is for skilled reading, the acquisition process for reading involves the child becoming aware of the alphabetic principle underlying printed language.

To discover whether children could be classified according to how much they relied on sight-word versus decoding strategies in word identification, we administered lists of words to read to a group of 90 Grade 2 children and 89 Grade 3 children. One list comprised exception words, like *laugh, there*, and *knife*, and another comprised nonwords like *pilk, skep*, and *winsup*. We subjected the data to cluster analyses, which identifies groupings of children in terms of levels of performance on the two tests. Four groups emerged at each grade. One, which contained about half of the children, comprised children who were above average on both lists (we refer to this groups as HB, high on both lists). In another, with around 13% of cases, the children were well below average on both lists (LB, low on both). Then there were two "cross-over" groups. In one of these, the children, 20% in Grade 2 and 26% in Grade 3, were average for exception words but well below average for nonwords (we can call these children PD, for poor decoders, remembering, however, that the LB group contains poor decoders too). The other, 13% and 16% in Grades 2 and 3, respectively, showed the opposite pattern: average or better for nonwords, below average for exception words (PS, for poor sight-word readers). For both grades, these clusters accounted for around 85% of the variance in the measures. Extracting another, fifth, cluster, did not increase the variance explained by a useful amount.

When we examined the reading comprehension of the four groups we found, not surprisingly, that in both Grades 2 and 3 the HB children performed best and the LB children worst. I say "not surprisingly" because even though our groups were defined on the basis of identification of isolated words, it is known that much of the variance in reading comprehension is attributable to word-level identification processes; see Byrne and Fielding-Barnsley (1995) for evidence and discussion, and recall Hoover and Gough's (1990) "simple view" of reading. LB children were also the poorest performers on our measures of phonemic awareness, which were matching spoken words for their final phonemes, as in *bud* and *mad*, and eliding the first consonant from spoken words, as in saying *stop* without the *s*. This pattern further confirms that good word identification skills underlie good reading comprehension, and that poor decoding (and in this case sight-word recognition) skills are accompanied by low levels of phonemic awareness.

The cross-over groups, PD and PS, need to be considered grade by grade. In Grade 2, their reading comprehension levels lay between the HB and LB groups. When we compared the groups with each other, we found that the children who were relatively better at reading exception words, the PD group, were the superior comprehenders and just about average for the 90 children in the sample. The PS children were almost 1 SD below the average for the sample. The PD children were also faster readers than the PS children, and also on the sample average. This tells us that at Grade 2 (around seven years of age in Australia), a reasonable stock of sight words serves children adequately, even if they are not good decoders. In contrast, in Grade 2 adequate decoding skills that are not matched by adequate sight word stocks produces readers who are slow and who are below average in reading comprehension.

Things change in Grade 3, however. Now the PS children were a little above average in reading comprehension, and about half a standard deviation above the PD children (whose standard score was –0.3). The PS children were still rather slow (.8 of a SD below the sample mean). Interestingly, these children's actual exception word reading, though low relative to their nonword reading, was only a little over half a standard deviation below the sample mean, and their nonword reading was almost half a standard deviation above the mean. In contrast, the Grade 2 PS children had scores of –1.1 SD and about average (+.1 SD) for exception and nonword reading, respectively. In other words, the Grade 3 children still showed the relative discrepancy that defines them as PS, but were higher in absolute level than their Grade 2 counterparts, as if adequate second-grade decoding skills were producing rather better readers in third grade, both in comprehension and in individual word identification.

In Grade 3, the PD children had a reading comprehension mean lower than the PS children, as noted in the previous paragraph, and almost as low as the LB children. In addition, their absolute scores on the two lists had declined by small amounts, suggesting a decline not only in comprehension but also in word identification. Apparently, poor decoding skills in Grade 2 give rise to problems in Grade 3.

The interpretation of these data is clouded by the fact that it is cross-sectional. So we retested these same children a year later, when the original second graders were in third grade and the third graders in fourth. The overall picture was strikingly similar to that shown by the cross-sectional analysis. The reading comprehension data for both Grade 2/3 comparisons, cross-sectional and longitudinal, are shown in Fig. 5.3.

For both comparisons, there is an interaction between group and grade, with the PS children improving both absolutely and relative to the PD children across the grades. Thus our earlier conclusion—that poor decoding skills that are accompanied by reasonable stocks of sight words can serve a child in Grade 2 but begin to fail the child by Grade 3—is confirmed by the more stringent test provided by longitudinal data.

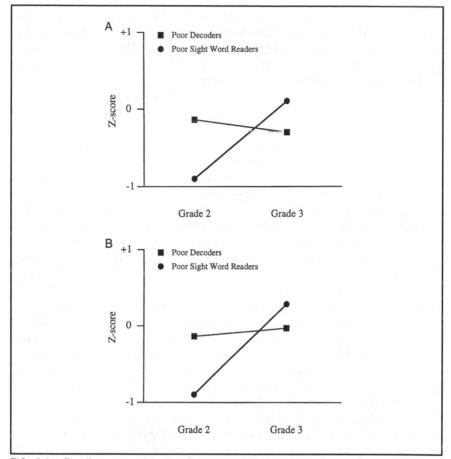

FIG. 5.3.   Reading comprehension (in z-scores) for poor decoders and poor sight-word readers: (A) cross-sectional comparison; (B) longitudinal comparison.

The Grade 3 PD and PS children who were retested in Grade 4 did not improve in reading comprehension, with levels almost identical to their third-grade ones. Thus there remained about half a standard deviation separating the two groups, favouring the better decoders (group PS). The LB children stayed very much the poorest comprehenders in the longitudinal analyses as well as continuing to score lowest on the tests of phonemic awareness and on word and nonword identification. This result again confirms the stability of relative standing across time and the co-occurrence of low levels of reading and of phonemic awareness.

All in all, these data point to serious consequences for a failure to become secure in decoding early in school. These consequences can be masked temporarily for those children who have managed to acquire an average reading vocabulary. However, in later elementary school grades, starting in Grade 3 in our sample, these children's difficulties begin to surface.

In explaining these trends, particularly the PS/PD comparison, I can do no better than quote our original version. We refer to "the changing demands on readers in the first years of schooling. The controls on vocabulary difficulty and diversity and the prevalent use of informative pictures in evidence in most school reading books would encourage reading from memory with a relatively small stock of sight words and picture-based recall. It is also the case that the most frequent words in first school books are often irregular. Freebody (1983) ... has shown that of the 182 most frequent words, accounting for 75% of all usage in a large corpus of materials written for use in the first three years of school (i.e., until the end of Grade 2), 93, or 51.1%, were irregularly spelled ... In contrast, in the corpus of school texts for Grades 3–9 collected by Carroll, Davies, and Richman (1971), it takes 1,266 different words to account for 75% of running text, and only 35% of these are irregularly spelled. Thus, the words that perform heavy duty in the early reading books do so to a decreasing extent as grade level increases and as growing numbers of middle-frequency, more regularly spelled words appear" (Byrne et al., 1992, p.150). Children who are ill-equipped to find their own way through this expanding (if not exploding) print vocabulary, that is children with a poor grasp of the alphabetic principle and poor decoding skills, face an uphill struggle. Children who have mastered the basic alphabetic code seem destined to enjoy a smoother journey through their schooling.

CHAPTER SUMMARY

Data we have collected were examined for the light they shed on individual differences in acquisition of the alphabetic principle. Verbal IQ, as measured via receptive vocabulary, was already related to phonemic awareness by age four, but it had little subsequent independent effect on the development of word-identification processes. Verbal IQ, however, related to reading comprehension when it was measured in Grades 2 and 3. It appears therefore that the primary influence of verbal ability is on higher-level reading processes. In our samples of children, its role in the acquisition of the alphabetic principle and the development of decoding was brief and limited.

Children's ability to recognise rhyming relations among words contributed to early phonemic awareness, perhaps by providing a focus on the form as opposed to the meaning of words. Later in schooling, rhyming skill (measured in preschool) made an independent contribution to explaining variance in spelling and in the reading of irregularly spelled words. Early rhyme appreciation may therefore contribute to the development of orthographic knowledge. One reason for this could be that words that are irregular at the phoneme-grapheme level exhibit more consistency at the rime level, as *night, light*, and *fright* illustrate.

Girls were more secure in letter knowledge and in an appreciation of print conventions at the preschool and kindergarten levels, and the preschool data showed an advantage for girls in the structured decoding test. However, there were no detectable sex differences in phonemic awareness, and none in word identification skills or reading comprehension during the school years. Overall, therefore, our data provided only limited support for the belief that girls outperform boys in literacy development; an early advantage for girls in print and letter awareness did not translate into later superiority at either word- or text-level reading processes.

Preschool children from families with a history of marked reading problems appear to be compromised in phonological awareness, letter knowledge, and familiarity with the conventions of printed language. In a substantial minority of our sample, phonemic awareness did not develop in response to an instructional programme, though the majority did improve. However, once the foundations for discovery of the alphabetic principle *are* in place, at-risk children appear to advance to decoding in the same way as normal children.

A project in which preschools were provided with the instructional programme *Sound Foundations* presented an opportunity to compare more and less intense instruction in phonemic awareness. Children in the original evaluation study, taught in small groups with closely monitored progress, made more substantial gains than children in the later study, taught in larger groups where the opportunity for monitoring was limited.

In a study motivated by questions about reading strategies in early school grades, it was found that early establishment of decoding skill is important for reading development. Children who had reasonable stock of "sight words" but who were poor decoders appeared to be progressing adequately in second grade but by third grade had begun to lag in text-level reading processes. In contrast, children who were average decoders but lacked average levels of sight words made gains in reading comprehension from second to third grades. Children who had low levels of both decoding and sight word skills were compromised throughout in higher-level reading processes.

CHAPTER SIX

Conclusions and implications

SUMMARY OF MAJOR FINDINGS AND CONCLUSIONS

The fact about writing systems that has been the centrepiece of this monograph is that orthographies are multiple codes on language. An alphabet, for example, not only systematically records the phonemes of language but also systematically records larger units of sound, such as syllables, and units of meaning, such as morphemes and words. Readers could in principle operate at any of these levels, each making different demands on phonological awareness, on decoding processes, and on memory.

We saw in Chapter 1 that adults could learn to read a novel writing system that marked the phonetic features of voicing and place without realising that the system did so. Thus, using a system and understanding its basic mapping of language are not the same thing. Failure to grasp the basic mapping limits the reader's ability to use the orthography productively. Much of the remainder of the book was concerned with the question of whether the same situation may hold for children learning to read English. That is, might children learn to read English words and yet not come to understand the alphabetic principle, thereby hampering their ability to read newly encountered words?

One a priori reason for expecting that this kind of learning could occur is the observation that young children do not appear to have conscious access to the phonemic organisation of the speech stream. To be concrete, we showed that close to three-quarters of children beginning school, although perfectly competent speakers of the language, could not reliably judge that two words, *pig* and *pool*, for instance, began with the same phoneme. Under those circumstances, it might not be surprising that they would not understand why *pig* and *pool* are written with the same first letter. This would not block their learning to read the words, but it would interfere with their grasp of the basic mapping of the print sequences onto the speech sequences. This, in turn, would mean that progress in reading could only be made as more and more words were committed to memory. Print could not become self-pronouncing.

A second a priori reason to think that children might miss seeing the alphabetic principle underlying English writing is their early assumption that printed language will reflect meaning in a fairly direct way. Given that we have already agreed that writing not only reflects phonological structure but also morphological and word structure, children will indeed find a consistent mapping of print onto meaning if they are of a mind to look for it.

Nevertheless, all of these potential barriers to discovering the alphabetic principle may crumble in the face of actual print experience. It may be enough to learn a few words to trigger insights into how letters represent language. To caricature the situation: A child who learns to read *dog* and *den* may ponder why each has three letters and why each starts with the same letter. The answers, that each has three phonemes and that each has the same initial phoneme, would come quickly to the child with a suitably tuned and prepared mind. The alphabetic code would thereby be cracked. If a few words is not enough, a hundred might be, or a thousand.

But experience with print alone might not in fact be sufficient to start this cascade of insights into alphabetic writing. Our evidence, indeed, suggests that it is not. First, in experiments in which children learned to read print-speech pairs systematically arranged to reveal letter-phoneme correspondences, children clung to the hypothesis that writing reflects meaning, in particular that it honours the morphological structure of language. They missed seeing that print also represents phonological structure. Second, even when a morphological analysis of a word's elements is not available, children still fail to recognise that English is fundamentally phonographic. They failed to learn letter-phoneme correspondences, just as our adult subjects had failed to learn "letter"-phonetic feature correspondences.

Evidence from other groups supports our claim that children can learn stocks of words without understanding the alphabetic principle well enough to be able to read novel words reliably. The strength of that evidence is that it is based on reasonably large word sets, and is set in real classrooms and clinics.

If children lack phonemic awareness, can they be taught it? If children do not unerringly induce the alphabetic principle as they learn to read words, can it be brought to their attention? These questions arise naturally from the evidence just presented. The questions are linked because it is proposed that one impediment to discovery of the alphabetic principle is a lack of phonemic awareness. The answer to both questions is a clear yes. In small-scale experiments and in a larger-scale classroom evaluation project we showed, first, that preschool children could be taught to analyse spoken words into their constituent phonemes. Second, we showed that providing children with this basic insight helped them learn to decode, as long as it was paired with relevant letter knowledge. Neither phonemic awareness nor letter knowledge by themselves supported early signs of decoding skill. It was the combination that was crucial.

Our classroom evaluation of a programme to teach phonemic awareness showed that the intervention fostered aspects of reading development besides decoding, including reading comprehension and engagement with books. Many of these effects were small, but against a background of an education system that endorses teaching letter-phoneme correspondences and over a time span that has extended out four years from the preschool intervention, it is perhaps surprising, and encouraging, that any effects were detectable at all.

Other data from our group confirmed that a good working knowledge of the alphabetic principle, indexed by decoding skills, stands the child in good stead during the early school years. Sometimes the difficulties engendered by poor decoding ability are not evident at first. As long as children have adequate word-level print-speech links, as indexed by reading of irregularly spelled words, their reading comprehension is also adequate. But in time, in our samples by Grade 3, decoding deficiencies begin to take their toll on higher-level reading tasks as well as on word-level ones.

Finally, we considered individual differences in children's acquisition of the alphabetic principle and subsequent (and consequent) decoding ability. Verbal IQ and sex had rather limited influence on these early stages of literacy development, but it was troubling to report that among children from families with a history of dyslexia there was a disproportionally high number who failed to achieve satisfactory levels of phonemic awareness despite intensive instruction. Why this is so, and what can be done about it, remain important questions for future research.

EDUCATIONAL IMPLICATIONS

I believe that the implications for literacy instruction are obvious and straightforward. In a nutshell, *if we want children to understand the alphabetic principle underpinning English orthography, we should tell them about it*. We should not rely on them fathoming the system for themselves. Why do we want them to understand the alphabetic principle? So that they can become independent readers What does "telling them" mean? First, making sure that they understand that spoken language separates into phonemes. Second, making sure that they realise that there is a limited number of phonemes and that they combine and recombine to create all the words of the language. Third, making sure that they realise that these phonemes are the objects that the elements of the writing system, the letters, represent. Fourth, making sure that they know which letters represent which phonemes.

Where does this embarrassingly brief paragraph leave us in terms of the debate about the best ways to teach reading?[1] Rather than comment on particular programmes with which I am familiar, I prefer to suggest some general ways of evaluating teaching methods and approaches. Most obviously, the previous paragraph says that instruction about the phonemic organisation of spoken language should be part of any programme. Approaches that neglect to include this, either by oversight or because of a view that "breaking whole (natural) language into bite-size, abstract little pieces" (Goodman, 1986, p.7) harms reading development, are negligent. Second, it says that letter knowledge is not a proxy for phonemic awareness. Teaching letters is a part of just about every reading curriculum that I am aware of, and rightly so. But letter knowledge unsupported by an understanding of the role in speech of phonemes, the letters' linguistic associates, is not a stable platform for embarking on a career as a little decoder. Letter knowledge and phonemic awareness should be coupled.

Thus, reading instruction programmes can be valued according to the degree to which they provide information about the foundations of the alphabetic principle, phonemic awareness and letter knowledge, and the way these foundations are linked.

The delivery of these well-founded programmes can also be judged on how effective they are in instilling an understanding of the alphabetic principle in each child in the class. We saw that less intensively delivered instruction leaves some children in the dark about phonemic structure. Given the evidence for the importance of phonemic awareness that we have surveyed, this is to be regretted.

The goal of reaching every child necessarily entails some form of assessment of these foundations, formal or informal but valid. Until assessment is a routine part of reading education in these crucial early stages, we can be accused of failing to do our best by children. Teachers and programmes that use targeted evaluation of children's progress and, of course, have plans to deal with children who are failing to achieve critical insights are to be valued.

There is another measure that we can use to evaluate instructional programmes. It is the degree to which they might obscure the alphabetic principle. Not just neglect it, obscure it. How could they do so? By further encouraging children to believe that they are on the right track in assuming that print basically represents meaning. Of course, print *does* represent meaning. But fundamentally, print represents phonological structures. However, if the data and analyses in Chapter 2 are to be trusted, children start out with a different view, that morphology is the currency of writing. So programmes that sanction the response "doggie" for *dog*, or worse "Fido" for *dog*, or worse still "doggie" on one occasion and "Fido" on another, may lead children further away from the alphabetic principle by providing frank confirmation of the hypothesis that meaning is the bottom line of writing. Such programmes may do this even if in other parts they encourage children to notice the role of letters in representing sounds (so-called "grapho-phonic cues"), because then the child has to deal with conflicting information about the basic currency of the system. We know very little about how a child might resolve this kind of conflict.

What needs to be juggled, therefore, are the requirements that reading instruction is sufficiently engaging to keep children on task and that it is sufficiently explicit about the important things to make it worthwhile staying on task. It would be most surprising if anyone who has made an honest effort to develop a reading programme, whatever that person's basic persuasion about how reading ought to be taught, did not have something to contribute to that juggling act.

BEYOND THE ALPHABETIC PRINCIPLE

We have been primarily concerned with the discovery of the alphabetic principle. We have looked at that process in a fair amount of detail, including how it might best be taught. But we have gone beyond a strict definition of the alphabetic principle in employing data on decoding and word identification in general, as anticipated at the beginning of Chapter 1. At the same time, we have given less consideration to the fine details of teaching decoding skills. We have just seen, in the evaluation project, that children who are taught the foundations of alphabetic orthography in phonemic structure become better decoders, and have assumed that these children were better placed than others to profit from the reading instruction provided by their schools. But exactly how children move from the alphabetic principle to productive decoding has remained largely outside the scope of this monograph. Put another way, we acknowledged early that the alphabetic principle and decoding were not one and the same thing. In fact, we saw that achieving phonemic awareness and relevant letter knowledge were necessary *but not sufficient* for decoding (see, for example, Table 4.2 and the surrounding discussion). The *necessity* part of this formula has permitted us to use decoding as a sign of the presence of the alphabetic principle. But the *not sufficiency* part implies that something is needed on top of the alphabetic principle to produce a successful decoder. It is just that we have not pursued the details of that something with determination.

Others have. Cunningham (1990) and Hatcher et al. (1994) have produced evidence that explicit instruction in blending phonemes to form words yields benefits for apprentice readers. More recently, Ruth Fielding-Barnsley (1997) has shown that explicit decoding instruction assists even children who have high levels of phoneme awareness and letter knowledge in generalising from learned words to novel ones. In some ways, this is another story. But even that fragment of the story fits the fundamental implication of this monograph, that *if we want children to know something, we would be advised to teach it explicitly*. And that seems like a good place to stop.

NOTE

1. I say "embarrassing" because at the end of a book upwards of 60,000 words, the educational implications can be condensed into a single paragraph, nay, a single (italicised) sentence. Surely any thoughtful grandmother would have offered the same advice, at the beginning of the book. But on further reflection, it appears to me that the research effort exemplified by this book, an effort that has its modern beginnings in the seminal work of Isabelle Liberman, Donald Shankweiler, Ignatius Mattingly and Alvin Liberman in the USA and Lynette Bradley and Peter Bryant in England, has said something new and important. It is in the list of things to tell children that the contribution resides. Grandmothers did not know about and could not tell their grandchildren about the phonemic organisation of the speech stream.

References

Adams, M.J. (1990). *Beginning to read: Thinking and learning about print.* Cambridge, MA: MIT Press.

Adams, M.J., & Bruck, M. (1993). Word recognition: The interface of educational policies and scientific research. *Reading and Writing, 5,* 113–139.

Atkinson, M. (1992). *Children's syntax: An introduction to principles and parameters theory.* Oxford: Blackwell.

Atkinson, R.L., Atkinson, R.C., Smith, E.E., Bem, D.J., & Nolen-Hoeksma, S. (1996). *Hilgard's introduction to psychology (12th ed.).* Fort Worth, TX: Harcourt Brace.

Ball, E.W., & Blachman, B.A. (1991). Does phoneme segmentation training in kindergarten make a difference in early word recognition and developmental spelling? *Reading Research Quarterly, 26,* 49–66.

Baron, J. (1977). Mechanisms for pronouncing printed words: Use and acquisition. In D. LaBerge & S.J. Samuels (Eds.), *Basic processes in reading: Perception and comprehension.* Hillsdale, NJ: Lawrence Erlbaum Associates Inc.

Baron, J. (1979). Orthographic and word-specific mechanisms in children's reading of words. *Child Development, 50,* 60–72.

Baron, J., & Strawson, C. (1976). Use of orthographic and word-specific knowledge in reading words aloud. *Journal of Experimental Psychology: Human Perception and Performance, 2,* 386–393.

Baron, J., & Treiman, R. (1980). Use of orthography in reading and learning to read. In J.F. Kavanagh & R.L. Venezky (Eds.), *Orthography, reading, and dyslexia* (pp. 171–189). Baltimore, MD: University Park Press.

Bloomfield, L., & Barnhart, C.L. (1961). *Let's read: A linguistic approach.* Detroit, MI: Wayne State University Press.

Bowey, J.A. (1995). Socioeconomic status differences in preschool phonological sensitivity and first-grade reading achievement. *Journal of Educational Psychology*, 87, 476–487.

Bowey, J.A., & Hansen, J. (1994). The development of orthographic rimes as units of word recognition. *Journal of Experimental Child Psychology*, 58, 134–159.

Bradley, L., & Bryant, P.E. (1983). Categorising sounds and learning to read—A causal connection. *Nature*, 301, 419–421.

Bradley, L., & Bryant, P.E. (1985) *Children's reading problems*. Oxford: Blackwell.

Brooks, L.R. (1977). Visual pattern in fluent word identification. In A.S. Reber & D.L. Scarborough (Eds.), *Toward a psychology of reading: The proceedings of the CUNY conference* (pp. 143–181). Hillsdale, NJ: Lawrence Erlbaum Associates Inc.

Bruck, M. (1990). Word-recognition skills of adults with childhood diagnoses of dyslexia. *Developmental Psychology*, 26, 439–454.

Bryant, P.E., Bradley, L., Maclean, M., & Crossland, J. (1989). Nursery rhymes, phonological skills and reading. *Journal of Child Language*, 16, 407–428.

Bryant, P.E., & Impey, L. (1986). The similarities between normal readers and developmental and acquired dyslexics. *Cognition*, 24, 121–137.

Byrne, B. (1984). On teaching articulatory phonetics via an orthography. *Memory and Cognition*, 12, 181–189.

Byrne, B. (1992). Studies in the acquisition procedure for reading: Rationale, hypotheses, and data. In P.B. Gough, L.C. Ehri & R. Treiman (Eds.), *Reading acquisition* (pp. 1–34). Hillsdale, NJ: Lawrence ErlbaumAssociates Inc.

Byrne, B. (1995). Individual differences, instruction, and the way ahead. *Issues in Education*, 1, 71–75.

Byrne, B. (1996). The learnability of the alphabetic principle: Children's initial hypotheses about how print represents spoken language. *Applied Psycholinguistics*, 17, 401–426.

Byrne, B., & Carroll, M. (1989). Learning artificial orthographies: Further evidence of a nonanalytic acquisition procedure. *Memory and Cognition*, 17, 311–317.

Byrne, B., & Fielding-Barnsley, R. (1989). Phonemic awareness and letter knowledge in the child's acquisition of the alphabetic principle. *Journal of Educational Psychology*, 81, 313–321.

Byrne, B., & Fielding-Barnsley, R. (1990). Acquiring the alphabetic principle: A case for teaching recognition of phoneme identity. *Journal of Educational Psychology*, 82, 805–812.

Byrne, B., & Fielding-Barnsley, R. (1991a). Evaluation of a program to teach phonemic awareness to young children. *Journal of Educational Psychology*, 83, 451–455.

Byrne, B., & Fielding-Barnsley, R. (1991b). *Sound foundations*. Sydney, Australia: Peter Leyden Educational Publishers.

Byrne, B., & Fielding-Barnsley, R. (1993a). Evaluation of a program to teach phonemic awareness to young children: A 1-year follow-up. *Journal of Educational Psychology*, 85, 104–111.

Byrne, B., & Fielding-Barnsley, R. (1993b). Recognition of phoneme invariance by beginning readers: Confounding effects of global similarity. *Reading and Writing*, 5, 315–324.

Byrne, B., & Fielding-Barnsley, R. (1995). Evaluation of a program to teach phonemic awareness to young children: A 2- and 3-year follow-up and a new preschool trial. *Journal of Educational Psychology, 87,* 488–503.

Byrne, B., Fielding-Barnsley, R., Ashley, L., & Larsen, K. (1997). Assessing the child's and the environment's contribution to reading acquisition: What we know and what we don't know. In B. Blachman (Ed.), *Foundations of reading acquisition and dyslexia: Implications for early intervention* (pp.265–285). Mahwah, NJ: Lawrence Erlbaum Associates Inc.

Byrne, B., Freebody, P., & Gates, A. (1992). Longitudinal data on the relations of word-reading strategies to comprehension, reading time, and phonemic awareness. *Reading Research Quarterly, 27,* 141–151.

Byrne, B., & Shea, P. (1979). Semantic and phonetic memory codes in beginning readers. *Memory and Cognition, 7,* 333–338.

Campbell, R., & Butterworth, B. (1985). Phonological dyslexia and dysgraphia in a highly literate subject: A developmental case with associated deficits of phonemic processing awareness. *Quarterly Journal of Experimental Psychology, 37A,* 435–475.

Cardon, L.R., Smith, S.D., Fulker, D.W., Kimberling, W.J., Pennington, B.F., & DeFries, J.C. (1994). Quantitative trait locus for reading disability on Chromosome 6. *Science, 266,* 276–279.

Cardoso-Martins, C. (1994). Rhyme perception: Global or analytic? *Journal of Experimental Child Psychology, 57,* 26–41.

Carey, S. (1982). Semantic development: The state of the art. In E. Wanner & L.R. Gleitman (Eds.), *Language acquisition: The state of the art* (pp. 347–389). Cambridge: Cambridge University Press.

Carr, P. (1993). *Phonology.* London: Macmillan.

Carroll, J.B., Davies, P., & Richman, B. (1971). *The American heritage word frequency book.* Boston, MA: Houghton Mifflin.

Castles, A., & Coltheart, M. (1993). Varieties of developmental dyslexia. *Cognition, 47,* 149–180.

Chall, J.S. (1967). *Learning to read: The great debate.* New York: McGraw-Hill.

Clay, M. (1975). *The early detection of reading difficulties: A diagnostic survey.* Auckland, New Zealand: Heinemann.

Coltheart, M., Curtis, B., Atkins, P., & Haller, M. (1993). Models of reading aloud: Dual-route and parallel-distributed-processing approaches. *Psychological Review, 100,* 589–608.

Coltheart, M., Davelaar, E., Jonasson, J.T., & Besner, D. (1977). Access to the internal lexicon. In S. Dornic (Ed.), *Attention and performance VI* (pp. 535–555). Hillsdale, NJ: Lawrence Erlbaum Associates Inc.

Coltheart, V., & Leahy, J. (1992). Children's and adults' reading of nonwords: Effects of regularity and consistency. *Journal of Experimental Psychology: Learning, Memory, and Cognition, 18,* 718–729.

Conrad, R. (1964). Acoustic confusions in immediate memory. *British Journal of Psychology, 55,* 75–84.

Cossu, G., Shankweiler, D., Liberman, I.Y., & Gugliotta, M. (1995). Visual and phonological determinants of misreadings in a transparent orthography. *Reading and Writing, 7,* 237–256.

Crowley, T., Lynch, J., Siegel, J., & Piau, J. (1995). *The design of language: An introduction to descriptive linguistics.* Auckland, New Zealand: Longman Paul.

Cunningham, A.E. (1990). Explicit versus implicit instruction in phonemic awareness. *Journal of Experimental Child Psychology, 50,* 429–444.

Cunningham, A.E., & Stanovich, K.E. (1990). Assessing print exposure and orthographic skill in children: A quick measure of reading experience. *Journal of Educational Psychology, 82*, 733–740.

Cutler, A., Mehler, J., Norris, D., & Segui, J. (1986). The syllable's differing role in the segmentation of French and English. *Journal of Memory and Language, 25*, 385–400.

DeFrancis, J. (1989). *Visible speech: The diverse oneness of writing systems.* Honolulu: University of Hawaii Press.

DeFries, J.C., & Gillis, J.J. (1991). Etiology of reading deficits in learning disabilities: Quantitative genetic analysis. In J.E. Obrzut & G.W. Hynd (Eds.), *Neuropsychological foundations of learning disabilities: A handbook of issues, methods, and practice.* Orlando, FL: Academic Press.

Dowker, A., & Pinto, G. (1993). Phonological devices in poems by English and Italian children. *Journal of Child Language, 20*, 697–706.

Ehri, L.C. (1992). Reconceptualizing the development of sight word reading and its relationship to recoding. In P.B. Gough, L.C. Ehri, & R. Treiman (Eds.), *Reading acquisition* (pp. 107–143). Hillsdale, NJ: Lawrence Erlbaum Associates Inc.

Ehri, L.C., & Wilce, L.S. (1985). Movement into reading: Is the first stage of printed word learning visual or phonetic? *Reading Research Quarterly, 20*, 163–179.

Felzen, E., & Anisfeld, M. (1970). Semantic and phonetic relations in the false recognition of words by third- and sixth-grade children. *Developmental Psychology, 3*, 163–168.

Ferreiro, E. (1985). Literacy development: A psychogenetic perspective. In D.R. Olson, N. Torrance, & A. Hildyard (Eds.), *Literacy, language, and learning: The nature and consequences of reading and writing* (pp. 217–228). Cambridge: Cambridge University Press.

Ferreiro, E. (1986). The interplay between information and assimilation in beginning literacy. In W.H. Teale & E. Sulzby (Eds.), *Emergent literacy: Writing and reading* (pp. 15–49). Norwood, NJ: Ablex.

Fielding-Barnsley, R. (1997). Explicit instruction in decoding benefits children high in phonemic awareness and alphabet knowledge. *Scientific Studies of Reading, 1*, 82–95.

Finney, S.A., Protopapas, A., & Eimas, P.D. (1996). Attentional allocation to syllables in American English. *Journal of Memory and Language, 35*, 893–909.

Foorman, B.R., & Francis, D.J. (1994). Exploring connections among reading, spelling, and phonemic segmentation during first grade. *Reading and Writing, 6*, 65–91.

Foorman, B.R., Francis, D.J., Novy, D.M., & Liberman, D. (1991). How letter-sound instruction mediates progress in first-grade reading and spelling. *Journal of Educational Psychology, 83*, 456–469.

Fowler, A.E. (1991). How early phonological development might set the stage for phoneme awareness. In S. Brady & D. Shankweiler (Eds.), *Phonological processes in literacy: A tribute to Isabelle Y. Liberman* (pp. 97–118). Hillsdale, NJ: Lawrence Erlbaum Associates Inc.

Fox, B., & Routh, D.K. (1975). Analyzing spoken language into words, syllables, and phonemes: A developmental study. *Journal of Psycholinguistic Research, 4*, 331–342.

Freebody, P. (1983). *The vocabulary of first school books: Statistical and semantic analyses*. Unpublished manuscript, University of New England, Armidale, New South Wales, Australia.

Freebody, P., & Byrne, B. (1988). Word-reading strategies in elementary school children: Relations to comprehension, reading time, and phonemic awareness. *Reading Research Quarterly, 23*, 441–453.

Gilger, J.W., Pennington, B.F., & DeFries, J.C. (1991). Risk for reading disability as a function of parental history in three family studies. *Reading and Writing, 3*, 205–218.

Gold, E.M. (1967). Language identification in the limit. *Information and Control, 16*, 447–474.

Goodman, K.S. (1986). *What's whole about whole language: A parent-teacher guide*. Portsmouth, NH: Heinemann.

Goodman, K.S., & Goodman, Y.M. (1979). Learning to read is natural. In L.B. Resnick & P.A. Weaver (Eds.), *Theory and practice of early reading* (Vol. 1, pp. 137–154). Hillsdale, NJ: Lawrence Erlbaum Associates Inc.

Goswami, U., & Bryant, P.E. (1990). *Phonological skills and learning to read*. Hove, UK: Lawrence Erlbaum Associates Ltd.

Goswami, U., & Bryant, P.E. (1992). Rhyme, analogy, and children's reading. In P.B. Gough, L.C. Ehri, & R. Treiman (Eds.), *Reading acquisition* (pp. 49–63). Hillsdale, NJ: Lawrence Erlbaum Associates Inc.

Gough, P.B., Juel, C., & Griffith, P.L. (1992). Reading, spelling, and the orthographic cipher. In P.B. Gough, L.C. Ehri, & R. Treiman (Eds.), *Reading acquisition* (pp. 35–48). Hillsdale, NJ: Lawrence Erlbaum Associates Inc.

Gough, P.B., & Walsh, M.A. (1991). Chinese, Phoenicians, and the orthographic cipher of English. In S. Brady & D. Shankweiler (Eds.), *Phonological processes in literacy: A tribute to Isabelle Y. Liberman* (pp. 119–209). Hillsdale, NJ: Lawrence Erlbaum Associates Inc.

Hatcher, P., Hulme, C., & Ellis, A.W. (1994). Ameliorating early reading failure by integrating the teaching of reading and phonological skills: The phonological linkage hypothesis. *Child Development, 65*, 41–57.

Hoover, W.A., & Gough, P.B. (1990). The simple view of reading. *Reading and Writing, 2*, 127–160.

Johnston, P.H. (1985). Understanding reading disability. *Harvard Educational Review, 55*, 153–177.

Juel, C. (1988). Learning to read & write: A longitudinal study of 54 children from first through fourth grades. *Journal of Educational Psychology, 80*, 437–447.

Kaye, J. (1989). *Phonology: A cognitive view*. Hillsdale, NJ: Lawrence Erlbaum Associates Inc.

Landsmann, L.T., & Levin, I. (1987). Writing in four- to six-year-olds: representation of semantic and phonetic similarities and differences. *Journal of Child Language, 14*, 127–144.

Larsen, K.P. (1994). *Irregular word reading, nonword reading, and print exposure*. Unpublished master's thesis, University of New England, Armidale, New South Wales, Australia.

Levin, I., & Korat, O. (1993). Sensitivity to phonological, morphological, and semantic cues in early reading and writing in Hebrew. *Merrill-Palmer Quarterly, 39*, 213–232.

Levin, J.R. (1992). On research in classrooms. *Mid-Western Educational Researcher, 5*, 2–6, 16.

Liberman, I.Y., & Liberman, A.M. (1992). Whole language versus code emphasis: Underlying assumptions and their implications for reading instruction. In P.B. Gough, L.C. Ehri, & R. Treiman (Eds.), *Reading acquisition* (pp. 343–366). Hillsdale, NJ: Lawrence Erlbaum Associates Inc.

Liberman, I.Y., Shankweiler, D.S., Fischer, F.W., & Carter, B. (1974). Explicit syllable and phoneme segmentation in the young child. *Journal of Experimental Child Psychology, 18,* 202–212.

Lindblom, B. (1986). On the origin and purpose of discreteness and invariance in sound patterns. In J.S. Perkell & D.H. Klatt (Eds.), *Invariance and variability in speech processes.* Hillsdale, NJ: Lawrence Erlbaum Associates Inc.

Lindblom, B., MacNeilage, P., & Studdert-Kennedy, M. (1983). Self-organizing processes and the explanation of phonological universals. In B. Butterworth, B. Comrie, & O. Dahl (Eds.), *Explanations for language universals* (pp. 181–203). The Hague, The Netherlands: Mouton.

Lovett, M.W., Borden, S.L., DeLuca, T., Lacerenza, L., Benson, N.J., & Brackstone, D. (1994). Treating the core deficits of developmental dyslexia: Evidence of transfer-of-learning following strategy- and phonologically based reading training programs. *Development Psychology, 30,* 805–822.

Lovett, M.W., Borden, S.L., Warren-Chaplin, P.M., Lacerenza, L., DeLuca, T., & Giovinazzo, R. (1996). Text comprehension training for disabled readers: An evaluation of reciprocal teaching and text analysis training programs. *Brain and Language, 54,* 447–480.

Lovett, M.W., Warren-Chaplin, P.M., Ransby, M.J., & Borden, S.L. (1990). Training the word recognition skills of reading-disabled children: Treatment and transfer effects. *Journal of Educational Psychology, 82,* 769–780.

Lundberg, I., Frost, J., & Petersen, O. (1988). Effects of an extensive program for stimulating phonological awareness in preschool children. *Reading Research Quarterly, 23,* 263–284.

Lundberg, I., & Tornéus, M. (1978). Nonreaders' awareness of the basic relationship between spoken and written words. *Journal of Experimental Child Psychology, 25,* 404–412.

Massaro, D. (1974). Perceptual units in speech recognition. *Journal of Experimental Psychology, 102,* 199–208.

Mehler, J., Dommergues, J., & Frauenfelder, U.H. (1981). The syllable's role in speech segmentation. *Journal of Verbal Learning and Verbal Behavior, 20,* 298–305.

Miller, G.A. (1977). *Spontaneous apprentices.* New York: Seabury Press.

Miller, G.A., & Nicely, P.E. (1955). Analysis of perceptual confusions among some English consonants. *Journal of the Acoustical Society of America, 27,* 338–352.

Miller, J. (1990). Speech perception. In D.N. Osherson & H. Lasnik (Eds.), *Language: An invitation to cognitive science* (Vol. 1, pp. 69–93). Cambridge, MA: MIT Press.

Morais, J., Cary, L., Alegria, J., & Bertelson, P. (1979). Does awareness of speech as a sequence of phones arise spontaneously? *Cognition, 7,* 323–331.

Morais, J., Cluytens, M., & Alegria, J. (1984). Segmentation abilities of dyslexics and normal readers. *Perceptual and Motor Skills, 58,* 221–222.

O'Connor, R.E., Jenkins, J.R., & Slocum, T.A. (1995). Transfer among phonological tasks in kindergarten: Essential instructional content. *Journal of Educational Psychology, 87,* 202–217.

Olson, R.K, Forsberg, H., & Wise, B. (1994). Genes, environment, and the development of orthographic skills. In V.W. Berninger (Ed.), *The varieties of orthographic knowledge I: Theoretical and developmental issues* (pp. 27–71). Dordrecht, The Netherlands: Kluwer.

Olson, R.K, Wise, B., Conners, F., Rack, J., & Fulker, D. (1989). Specific deficits in component reading and language skills: Genetic and environmental influences. *Journal of Learning Disabilities, 22,* 339–348.

Olson, R.K., Wise, B., Johnson, M., & Ring, J. (1997). The etiology and remediation of phonologically based word recognition and spelling disabilities: Are phonological deficits the "hole" story? In B. Blachman (Ed.), *Foundations of reading acquisition and dyslexia: Implications for early intervention* (pp.305–326). Mahwah, NJ: Lawrence Erlbaum Associates Inc.

Osherson, D.N., Stob, M., & Weinstein, S. (1985). *Systems that learn.* Cambridge, MA: MIT Press.

Pinker, S. (1979). Formal models of language learning. *Cognition, 7,* 217–283.

Pinker, S. (1990). Language acquisition. In D.N. Osherson & H. Lasnik (Eds.), *Language: An invitation to cognitive science* (Vol. 1, pp. 199–241). Cambridge, MA: MIT Press.

Plaut, D.C., McClelland, J.L., Seidenberg, M.S., & Patterson, K. (1996). Understanding normal and impaired reading: Computational principles in quasi-regular domains. *Psychological Review, 103,* 56–115.

Poser, W.J. (1994). [Review of the book *Mother of writing: The origin and development of a Hmong messianic script*]. *Phonology, 11,* 365–369.

Rack, J., Hulme, C., Snowling, M., & Wightman, J. (1994). The role of phonology in young children learning to read words: The direct-mapping hypothesis. *Journal of Experimental Child Psychology, 57,* 42–71.

Ratliff, M. (1996). The Pahawh Hmong script. In P.T. Daniels & W. Bright (Eds.), *The world's writing systems* (pp.619–624). Oxford: Oxford University Press.

Read, C. (1971). Pre-school children's knowledge of English phonology. *Harvard Educational Review, 41,* 1–34.

Rozin, P. (1976). The evolution of intelligence and access to the cognitive unconscious. In J.M. Sprague & A.N. Epstein (Eds.), *Progress in psychobiology and physiological psychology* (Vol 6, pp. 245–280). New York: Academic Press

Rozin, P., & Gleitman, L.R. (1977). The structure and acquisition of reading II: The reading process and the acquisition of the alphabetic principle. In A.S. Reber & D.L. Scarborough (Eds.), *Toward a psychology of reading: The proceedings of the CUNY conference* (pp. 55–141). Hillsdale, NJ: Lawrence Erlbaum Associates Inc.

Sampson, G. (1985). *Writing systems: A linguistic introduction.* London: Hutchinson.

Sattler, J.M. (1988). *Assessment of children (3rd ed.).* San Diego, CA: J.M. Sattler.

Scarborough, H.S. (1989). Prediction of reading disability from familial and individual differences. *Journal of Educational Psychology, 81,* 101–108.

Scarborough, H.S. (1991). Antecedents to reading disability: Preschool language development and literacy experiences of children from dyslexic families. *Reading and Writing, 3,* 219–234.

Schacter, D.L. (1987). Implicit memory: History and current status *Journal of Experimental Psychology: Learning, Memory, and Cognition, 13,* 501–518.

Seidenberg, M.S., & McClelland, J.L. (1989). A distributed, developmental model of word recognition and naming. *Psychological Review, 96,* 523–568.

Selkirk, E.O. (1984). On the major class features and syllable theory. In M. Aranoff & R.T. Oehrle (Eds.), *Language sound structure: Studies in phonology presented to Morris Halle by his teacher and students* (pp. 107–136). Cambridge, MA: MIT Press.

Seymour, P.H.K., & Elder, L. (1986). Beginning reading without phonology. *Cognitive Neuropsychology, 3,* 1 36.

Shankweiler, D.S., Liberman, I.Y., Mark, L.S., Fowler, C.A., & Fischer, F.W. (1979). The speech code and learning to read. *Journal of Experimental Psychology: Human Learning and Memory, 5,* 531–545.

Share, D.L. (1995). Phonological recoding and self-teaching: *sine qua non* of reading acquisition. *Cognition, 55,* 151–218.

Share, D.L., & Stanovich, K.E. (1995). Cognitive processes in early reading development: Accommodating individual differences into a model of acquisition. *Issues in Education, 1,* 1–57.

Shaywitz, B.A., Holford, T.R., Holohan, J.M., Fletcher, J.M., Stuebing, K.K., Francis, D.J., & Shaywitz, S.E. (1995). A Matthew effect for IQ but not for reading: Results from a longitudinal study. *Reading Research Quarterly, 30,* 894–906.

Shaywitz, B.A., Shaywitz, S.E., Pugh, K.R., Constable, R.T, Skudlarski, P., Fulbright, R.K., Bronen, R.A., Fletcher, J.M., Shankweiler, D.S., Katz, L., & Gore, J. (1995). Sex differences in the functional organization of the brain for language. *Nature, 373,* 607–609.

Shaywitz, S.E., Shaywitz, B.A., Fletcher, J.M., & Escobar, M.D. (1990). Prevalence of reading disability in boys and girls: Results of the Connecticut Longitudinal Study. *Journal of the American Medical Association, 264,* 998–1002.

Smalley, W.A., Vang, C.K., & Yang, G.Y. (1990). *Mother of writing: The origin and development of a Hmong messianic script.* Chicago, IL: University of Chicago Press.

Snowling, M. (1980). The development of grapheme-phoneme correspondence in normal and dyslexic readers. *Journal of Experimental Child Psychology, 29,* 294–305.

Snowling, M. (1987). *Dyslexia : a cognitive developmental perspective.* Oxford: Blackwell.

Snowling, M.J., Bryant, P.E., & Hulme, C. (1996). Theoretical and methodological pitfalls in making comparisons between developmental and acquired dyslexia: Some comments on A. Castles & M. Coltheart. *Reading and Writing, 8,* 443–451.

Spear-Swerling, L., & Sternberg, R.S. (1994). The road not taken: An integrative theoretical model of reading disability. *Journal of Learning Disabilities, 27,* 91–103.

Stanovich, K.E. (1986). Matthew effects in reading: Some consequences of individual differences in the acquisition of literacy. *Reading Research Quarterly, 21,* 360–407.

Stanovich, K.E., Cunningham, A.E., & Cramer, B.B. (1984). Assessing phonological awareness in kindergarten children: Issues of task comparability. *Journal of Experimental Child Psychology, 38,* 175–190.

Stanovich, K.E., Cunningham, A.E., & Freeman, D.J. (1984). Relation between early reading acquisition and word decoding with and without context. A longitudinal study of first-grade children. *Journal of Educational Psychology, 76,* 668–677.

Stanovich, K.E., Siegel, L.S., & Gottardo, A. (1997). Converging evidence for phonological and surface subtypes of reading disability. *Journal of Educational Psychology, 89,* 114–127.

Stothard, S., Snowling, M.J., & Hulme, C. (1996). Deficits in phonology but not dyslexic? *Cognitive Neuropsychology, 13,* 641–672.

Torgesen, J.K., Morgan, S.T., & Davis, C. (1992). Effects of two types of phonological awareness training on word learning in kindergarten children. *Journal of Educational Psychology, 84,* 364–370.

Treiman, R. (1984). Individual differences among children in reading and spelling styles. *Journal of Experimental Child Psychology, 38,* 463–477.

Treiman, R. (1985). Onsets and rimes as units of spoken syllables: Evidence from children. *Journal of Experimental Child Psychology, 39,* 161–181.

Treiman, R. (1993). *Beginning to spell: A study of first-grade children.* New York: Oxford University Press.

Treiman, R., & Baron, J. (1983). Phonemic-analysis training helps children benefit from spelling-sound rules. *Memory and Cognition, 11,* 382–389.

Treiman, R., & Breaux, A.M. (1982). Common phoneme and overall similarity relations among spoken syllables: Their use by children and adults. *Journal of Psycholinguistic Research, 11,* 569–598.

Treiman, R., Goswami, U., & Bruck, M. (1990). Not all nonwords are alike: Implications for reading development and theory. *Memory and Cognition, 18,* 559–567.

Treiman, R., & Zukowski, A. (1991). Levels of phonological awareness. In S. Brady & D. Shankweiler (Eds.), *Phonological processes in literacy: A tribute to Isabelle Y. Liberman* (pp. 67–83). Hillsdale, NJ: Lawrence Erlbaum Associates Inc.

Treiman, R., & Zukowski, A. (1996). Children's sensitivity to syllables, onsets, rimes, and phonemes. *Journal of Experimental Child Psychology, 61,* 193–215.

Tunmer, W.E., & Hoover, W.A. (1992). Cognitive and linguistic factors in learning to read. In P.B. Gough, L.C. Ehri, & R. Treiman (Eds.), *Reading acquisition* (pp. 175–214). Hillsdale, NJ: Lawrence Erlbaum Associates Inc.

Vellutino, F.R., & Scanlon, D.M. (1987). Phonological coding, phonological awareness, and reading ability: Evidence from a longitudinal and experimental study. *Merrill-Palmer Quarterly, 33,* 321–363.

Walley, A.C. (1993). The role of vocabulary development in children's spoken word recognition and segmentation ability. *Developmental Review, 13,* 286–350.

Whitehurst, G.J., Falco, F., Lonigan, C.J., Fischel, J.E., Valdez-Manchaca, M.C., & Caulfield, M. (1988). Accelerating language development through picture-book reading. *Developmental Psychology, 24,* 552–558.

Wimmer, H., & Hummer, P. (1990). How German-speaking first graders read and spell: Doubts on the importance of the logographic stage. *Applied Psycholinguistics, 4,* 349–368.

Wimmer, H., Landerl, K., Linortner, R., & Hummer, P. (1991). The relationship of phonemic awareness to reading acquisition: More consequence than precondition but still important. *Cognition, 40,* 219–249.

Wimmer, H., Landerl, K., & Schneider, W. (1994). The role of rhyme awareness in learning to read a regular orthography. *British Journal of Developmental Psychology, 12*, 469–484.

Woodcock, R.W. (1987). *Woodcock reading mastery tests-revised*. Circle Pines, MN: American Guidance Service.

Author index

Adams, M.J., 9, 61, 109
Alegria, J., 68, 114
Anisfeld, M., 66
Ashley, L., 62, 105
Atkins, P., 133
Atkinson, M., 16, 53
Atkinson, R.C., x
Atkinson, R.L., x

Ball, E.W., 102
Barnhart, C.L., 9
Baron, J., 102, 132
Bem, D.J., x
Benson, N.J., 104, 105
Bertelson, P., 114
Besner, D., 132
Blachman, B.A., 102
Bloomfield, L., 9
Borden, S.L., 104, 105
Bowey, J.A., 119, 122
Brackstone, D., 104, 105
Bradley, L., 6, 91, 93, 102, 108
Breaux, A.M., 112
Bronen, R.A., 110
Brooks, L.R., 14
Bruck, M., 9, 109, 119, 132

Bryant, P.E., 6, 91, 93, 102, 118, 119, 133
Butterworth, B., 62
Byrne, B., 11, 12, 15, 38, 39, 43, 49, 50, 53, 54, 55, 57, 58, 59, 62, 66, 68, 77, 79, 80, 81, 82, 83, 84, 85, 87, 95, 98, 99, 101, 105, 107, 111, 115, 117, 122, 127, 129, 131, 132, 133, 134, 137

Campbell, R., 62
Cardon, L.R., 113
Cardoso-Martins, C., 112
Carey, S., 52
Carr, P., 72
Carroll, J.B., 137
Carroll, M., 11, 12
Carter, B., 68, 69, 118
Cary, L., 114
Castles, A., 133
Caulfield, M., 115, 131
Chall, J.S., 61
Clay, M., 87
Cluytens, M., 68
Coltheart, M., 132, 133
Coltheart, V., 119

Subject index